HOW TO INTERPRET
FIRST JOHN

HOW TO INTERPRET
FIRST JOHN

DENNIS M. ROKSER

TRUE GRACE BOOKS
TACOMA, WA

TRUE
GRACE
BOOKS

First True Grace Books Edition, April 2024

How to Interpret First John

Copyright © 2024 by Dennis M. Rokser

Published by True Grace Books, Tacoma, WA.

Library of Congress Control Number: In Review

ISBN: 978-1-964184-08-1 (Paperback)

1. Bible. 2. Interpretation. 3. Epistles.

Originally published by Grace Gospel Press, 2015 (ISBN 978-1-939110-16-9)

All rights reserved. No portion of this publication may be reproduced, stored in a retrieval system, or transmitted in any form or by any means—electronic, mechanical, photocopy, recording, scanning, or other—except for brief quotations, without the prior written permission of the publisher.

All Scripture quotations, unless otherwise indicated, are taken from the New King James Version®. Copyright © 1982 by Thomas Nelson, Inc. Used by permission. All rights reserved.

Cover design by E Dane Rogers
Graphics by Canva, licensed use

Printed in the United States of America

2   4   6   8   10   9   7   5   3   1

As a pastor and Bible teacher for over 30 years, I have had the privilege of teaching verse by verse through a number of books from both the Old and New Testaments. Yet until more recently, I have found the epistle of 1 John to be very challenging to interpret. Apparently I am not alone as differences of opinion and theological controversy have marked the interpretation of this epistle. First John was written by the apostle John in approximately A.D. 90–95 and it consists of only five chapters and 105 verses. So why is this short book so exegetically challenging?

Amidst this controversy, Bible teachers have wrestled with and disagreed on primarily three pertinent questions:

1. Who are the recipients of this epistle?

2. What is the main subject and primary purpose of 1 John?

3. How do you interpret various difficult verses such as:

> 1 John 3:9: Whoever has been born of God does not sin, for His seed remains in him; and he cannot sin, because he has been born of God.

> 1 John 3:15: Whoever hates his brother is a murderer, and you know that no murderer has eternal life abiding in him.

> 1 John 5:16-17: If anyone sees his brother sinning a sin which does not lead to death,

> he will ask, and He will give him life for those who commit sin not leading to death. There is sin leading to death. I do not say that he should pray about that. 17 All unrighteousness is sin, and there is sin not leading to death.

In fact, the correct interpretation of 1 John has become a key factor and benchmark issue in the modern Lordship Salvation versus True Grace controversy that has rocked evangelical Christianity since the 1980s. Thus, I would like to offer some fresh interpretative insights and observations on 1 John. I trust these will encourage you in your study of God's Word as you sincerely search out its truth in Berean-like fashion (Acts 17:11). My purpose in writing this booklet is not to provide a verse-by-verse commentary on 1 John but to walk you, the reader, through some difficult and important issues regarding this epistle. In addition, this booklet is designed to provide some fresh exegetical observations and insights that have personally clarified the meaning of 1 John for me in a greater way and I trust they will for you as well. If you are willing to carefully consider these exegetical observations about 1 John as a whole and some of its more difficult passages, I believe you will see that they make tremendous interpretative sense and harmonize with the rest of Scripture. So read on!

Fresh Insights & Observations to Consider

SEVEN SIGNIFICANT QUESTIONS & FRESH OBSERVATIONS

1. WERE THE ORIGINAL RECIPIENTS OF THIS EPISTLE GENUINE BELIEVERS OR UNBELIEVERS, OR WERE THEY A MIXTURE OF BOTH?

While this is a simple question, it has resulted in several different answers and viewpoints, but they can be boiled down to two main perspectives.

a. First John is written to both true believers and unbelievers, though the latter claim to be Christians but are deceived.

This is the viewpoint of most pastors, teachers, and commentators, who view this epistle as a series of "tests" to discern the reality of a "Christian's" salvation. First John was supposedly written to provide the scriptural means and criteria to separate the wheat from the chaff—to separate those who *profess* to be Christians (but are not) from those who truly *possess* a saving relationship with Jesus Christ. Thus, the majority of interpreters view 1 John as having been written to a mixed audience of believers, who are genuinely saved, and unbelievers, who are not truly born again but are deceived in thinking they are genuine children of God.

b. First John is written only to believers, who are being swayed and influenced by false teachers.

This viewpoint regards 1 John as having been written to believers who were confused or in need of clarification about their daily fellowship with God. In addition, these believers were being influenced by unsaved, false teachers who held to a form of Gnostic heresy that denied the true person and finished work of Jesus Christ and that Jesus Christ did not come in the flesh. Thus, the apostle John wanted these dear believers to know afresh the truth about Jesus Christ and the importance of holding fast to sound doctrine. This was needed in order to walk in the light of God and His Word and have fellowship with God, resulting in obedience to God's will and love for the brethren.

Exegetical Observations on the Recipients of 1 John

Exegetically, the recipients of 1 John are clearly believers in Christ whom the apostle John is deeply concerned about in light of the influence and inroads of false Gnostic teachers. This is supported by several observations regarding the apostle John's identification of his readers.

First, we immediately see *the apostle John personally identify with his readers* as a fellow believer in Christ. At the very outset of the epistle, John uses the personal plural pronoun "we," including himself with his readers. Observe how John begins writing this epistle with "we" (referring to himself and the other apostles who saw Christ in the flesh) and then shifts to "you" (referring to his readers), as he refutes the Gnostic heresy that de-

Fresh Insights & Observations to Consider

nied Jesus Christ was fully human (i.e., flesh and blood. See 1 John 4:1-3; 5:6-8).

> 1 John 1:1-5: That which was from the beginning, which *we* [the apostles] have heard, which *we* [the apostles] have seen with our eyes, which *we* [the apostles] have looked upon, and *our* [the apostles] hands have handled, concerning the Word of life—2 the life was manifested, and *we* [the apostles] have seen, and bear witness, and declare to *you* [his readers] that eternal life [Jesus Christ] which was with the Father and was manifested to *us* [the apostles]—3 that which *we* [the apostles] have seen and heard *we* [the apostles] declare to you [his readers], that *you* [his readers] also may have fellowship with *us* [the apostles]; and truly *our* [the apostles] fellowship is with the Father and with His Son Jesus Christ. 4 And these things *we* [the apostles] write to you that your joy may be full. 5 This is the message which *we* [the apostles] have heard from Him and declare to *you* [his readers], that God is light and in Him is no darkness at all.

Observe that though the epistle begins with a "we" to "you" form of address, starting in verse 6 the two become blended so that the apostle John now personally identifies with his readers.

> 1 John 1:6-10: If we [John and his readers] say that we have fellowship with Him, and

walk in darkness, we [John and his readers] lie and do not practice the truth. 7 But if we [John and his readers] walk in the light as He is in the light, we [John and his readers] have fellowship with one another, and the blood of Jesus Christ His Son cleanses us [John and his readers] from all sin. 8 If we [John and his readers] say that we [John and his readers] have no sin, we [John and his readers] deceive ourselves, and the truth is not in us [John and his readers]. 9 If we [John and his readers] confess our sins, He is faithful and just to forgive us [John and his readers] our sins and to cleanse us [John and his readers] from all unrighteousness. 10 If we [John and his readers] say that we [John and his readers] have not sinned, we [John and his readers] make Him a liar, and His word is not in us [John and his readers].

John identifies himself fully and completely with his readers, who are fellow believers in Christ, not unbelievers. He makes no distinction or separation from them at all. Each of the false claims (1:6, 8, 10) and necessary conditions for fellowship with God (1:7, 9) apply equally to John and his readers. This identification with his Christian audience is further confirmed in the next 2 verses:

> 1 John 2:1-2: My little children, these things I [apostle John] write to you [his Christian readers], so that you [his Christian read-

ers] may not sin. And if anyone [Christian] sins, we [the apostle John and his Christian readers] have an Advocate with the Father, Jesus Christ the righteous. 2 And He Himself is the propitiation for our [John and his Christian readers] sins, and not for ours [John and his Christian readers] only but also for the whole world [those who are distinct from believers in Christ – the unbelieving world].

Though some Calvinists who embrace limited atonement interpret the "world" to mean the "world of the elect" and force their theology upon this passage, John's later usage of the term "world" in this same epistle destroys this notion.

> 1 John 5:19: *We* know that *we* are of God, and the whole *world* lies under the sway of the wicked one.

Note once again that there is a clear distinction between "we" (the redeemed) and the "world" (the unredeemed), just like in 1 John 2:2. The pronouns "we" and "us" continue to be used throughout the epistle by the apostle John as he identifies with his readers about their personal possession of eternal life, which only believers have.

> 1 John 2:25: And this is the promise that He has promised *us* [John and his Christian readers] — eternal life.

1 John 4:7: Beloved, let *us* [John and his Christian readers] love one another, for love is of God; and everyone who loves is born of God and knows God.

1 John 4:11 Beloved, if God so loved *us* [John and his Christian readers], *we* [John and his Christian readers] also ought to love one another.

1 John 4:19: *We* [John and his Christian readers] love Him because He first loved *us* [John and his Christian readers].

1 John 5:11: And this is the testimony: that God has given *us* [John and his Christian readers] eternal life, and this life is in His Son.

1 John 5:20: And *we* [John and his Christian readers] know that the Son of God has come and has given *us* [John and his Christian readers] an understanding, that *we* [John and his Christian readers] may know Him who is true; and *we* [John and his Christian readers] are in Him who is true, in His Son Jesus Christ. This is the true God and eternal life.

Could these statements possibly describe any unregenerate, unredeemed, unsaved unbeliever? No! But they certainly are true of any and all who have trusted in Jesus Christ as Savior. So John's personal identification with his readers strongly supports the conclusion that his audience consists of only believers in Christ.

Second, the fact that the original recipients of 1 John consisted of only believers in Christ is supported further by *the various descriptions of the readers* in this epistle. Observe these carefully:

> 1 John 2:1: *My little children*, these things I write to you, so that you may not sin. And if anyone sins, *we have an Advocate with the Father, Jesus Christ the righteous.*

Would you call the unsaved "little children" and then discuss with them about what happens "if" they "sin"? Never! For all have sinned and fall short of the glory of God (Rom. 3:23). But you would definitely discuss this with believers in Christ (Rom. 6:15).

> 1 John 2:7: *Brethren*, I write no new commandment to *you*, but an old commandment which *you* have had from the beginning.

Would you call the unsaved "brethren" in a spiritual sense? Never! For they have never been born again into the family of God. But you would refer to those who have been born again as "brethren" (James 1:18-19).

> 1 John 2:12: I write to you, *little children, because your sins are forgiven you for His name's sake.*

Would you ever tell the unsaved that their sins are forgiven, even though they have not yet trusted in Christ alone (Acts 10:43)? However, you would say this to those who have trusted in the Savior (Col. 2:13).

> 1 John 2:13-14: I write to you, *fathers, because you have known Him who is from the beginning*. I write to you, *young men, because you have overcome the wicked one*. I write to you, *little children, because you have known the Father*. 14 I have written to you, *fathers, because you have known Him who is from the beginning*. I have written to you, *young men, because you are strong, and the word of God abides in you, and you have overcome the wicked one*.

Would you address the unsaved in different stages of spiritual growth when they still lack spiritual life? Never! But you would address people this way who have been born again and now need to grow spiritually (1 Peter 1:23–2:3).

> 1 John 2:18: *Little children*, it is the last hour; and as you have heard that the Antichrist is coming, even now many antichrists have come, by which we know that it is the last hour.

> 1 John 2:21: I have not written to *you* because *you* do not know the truth, but *because you know it*, and that no lie is of the truth.

Would you describe the unsaved as those who know the truth? John stated this about his readers!

> 1 John 2:28: And now, *little children, abide in Him,* that when He appears, we may have confidence and not be ashamed before Him at His coming.

Would you command the unsaved to "abide" in Christ when they have not even been placed into Christ? Certainly not! But you would give these instructions to those who have been forgiven of all their sins (John 15:1-5).

> 1 John 3:1-2: Behold what manner of love the Father has bestowed on us, that we should be called *children of God!* Therefore the world (of the unsaved) does not know us, because it did not know Him. 2 *Beloved, now we are children of God*; and it has not yet been revealed what we shall be, but we know that when He is revealed, *we shall be like Him, for we shall see Him as He is.*

Would you describe the unsaved as "children of God"? No, you would call them "children of wrath," as Paul does in Ephesians 2:3. Instead, you would say to believers in Christ, "For we are all the children of God through faith in Christ Jesus" (Gal. 3:26).

> 1 John 3:13: Do not marvel, *my brethren,* if the world hates you.

> 1 John 3:18: *My little children,* let us not love in word or in tongue, but in deed and in truth.

1 John 3:21: *Beloved*, if our heart does not condemn us, we have confidence toward God.

1 John 4:1: *Beloved*, do not believe every spirit, but test the spirits, whether they are of God; because many false prophets have gone out into the world.

1 John 4:4: *You are of God, little children, and have overcome them,* because He who is in you is greater than he who is in the world.

1 John 5:13: These things I have written to *you who believe in the name of the Son of God,* that *you* [believers in Christ] *may know that you have eternal life*, and that *you* may continue to believe in the name of the Son of God.

1 John 5:19: *We* [fellow believers] *know that we* [fellow believers] *are of God*, and the whole world lies under the sway of the wicked one.

1 John 5:20: And *we* [fellow believers] *know that the Son of God has come and has given us an understanding*, that *we* [fellow believers] *may know Him who is true*; and *we* [fellow believers] *are in Him who is true*, in His Son Jesus Christ. This is the true God and eternal life.

1 John 5:21: *Little children*, keep yourselves from idols. Amen.

Throughout this epistle, the apostle John consistently and repeatedly uses descriptions and des-

Fresh Insights & Observations to Consider

ignations for his readers that identify them as believers in Jesus Christ. These believers are clearly born again and members of the family of God, who can now enjoy practical fellowship with God from day to day since 1 John and the rest of the Bible distinguish being a child of God and having fellowship with God.

Family of God	**Fellowship with God**
1. entered at a *point of time* when born again (John 1:12-13; 3:1-18; 1 John 3:2)	1. enjoyed in the *present* if a believer walks in the light (1 John 1:3-7)
2. true of *all* genuine believers in Christ (Gal. 3:26; 1 Jn. 5:1)	2. *not* true of all believers . . . "if" (1 John 1:5-10)
3. sins are *positionally / judicially* forgiven (Eph.1:7; Col. 2:13; 1 John 2:12)	3. sins may be *parentally* forgiven (1 John 1:9)
4. *faith* alone required (John 1:12; Gal. 3:26)	4. *faith* and *confession of sin* required (Heb. 11:6; 1 John 1:9)
5. evidenced by a *new nature* (2 Pt. 1:3-4), God's *chastisement* (Heb. 12:6-8), and becoming a *new creation* (2 Cor. 5:17)	5. evidenced by *obedience* to God's will (1 John 2:3-6) and *love* for other believers (1 John 2:7-11)

Third, John makes a *clear distinction between his readers and the unsaved false teachers* that were infiltrating their churches. Observe the change in pronouns from "we" to "they," which clearly distinguishes these two groups of people in 1 John.

> 1 John 2:18-20: Little children, it is the last hour; and as *you* [Christian readers] have heard that the Antichrist is coming, even now many antichrists have come, by which *we* [John and his Christian readers] know that it is the last hour. 19 *They* [the unsaved false teachers] went out from *us* [Christians], but they were not of *us* [Christians]; for if *they* [the false teachers] had been of *us* [Christians], *they* [the unsaved false teachers] would have continued with *us* [Christians]; but *they* [the unsaved false teachers] went out that they might be made manifest, that none of them were of us [agreed with what we as Christians believe about Christ]. But *you* [believers in contrast to the unsaved false teachers] have an anointing from the Holy One, and you [believers] know all things.

> 1 John 2:26: These things I have written to *you* [Christians] concerning *those* [the false teachers] who try to deceive *you* [believers].

> 1 John 4:4: You [believers] *are of God, little children,* and have overcome *them* [the unsaved false teachers], because He who is in *you* [believers] is greater than he who is in the world. *They* [the unsaved false

teachers] are of the world. Therefore *they* [the unsaved false teachers] speak as of the world, and the world hears them.

The apostle John is writing only to fellow believers in Christ. As he does so, he distinguishes these believers from the people he is warning about—the unsaved false teachers, who were seeking to doctrinally lead these believers astray from the truth about Jesus Christ.

Fourth, the original recipients of 1 John were fellow believers in Christ as seen by the similar descriptions given to the original readers of 2 John and 3 John. In his other two epistles, John uses identical or similar language to describe his readers as being believers, not unbelievers. Note the following:

2 John 1:1: The elder, to the elect lady and her children, whom I love in truth, and not only I, but also all those who have known the truth.

This lady (whether actual or figurative) is described as "elect"—a term used for a believer in Christ, along with her children.

2 John 1:2: because of the truth which abides in us and will be with us forever.

This clearly describes a believer but sounds very much like what John wrote in 1 John 2:21.

> 1 John 2:21: I have not written to you because you do not know the truth, but because you know it, and that no lie is of the truth.

Then John writes in 2 John:

> 2 John 1:3: Grace, mercy, and peace will be with you from God the Father and from the Lord Jesus Christ, the Son of the Father, in truth and love.

This is a typical first-century address to a believer, not an unbeliever. Then John writes,

> 2 John 1:4: I rejoiced greatly that I have found some of your children walking in truth, as we received commandment from the Father.

This sounds similar to 1 John 1:7:

> 1 John 1:7: But if we walk in the light as He is in the light, we have fellowship with one another, and the blood of Jesus Christ His Son cleanses us from all sin.

John continues:

> 2 John 1:5: And now I plead with you, lady, not as though I wrote a new commandment to you, but that which we have had from the beginning: that we love one another.

This is exactly what John wrote to believers in his first epistle:

> 1 John 2:7-10: Brethren, I write no new commandment to you, but an old commandment which you have had from the beginning. The old commandment is the word which you heard from the beginning. 8 Again, a new commandment I write to you, which thing is true in Him and in you, because the darkness is passing away, and the true light is already shining. 9 He who says he is in the light, and hates his brother, is in darkness until now. 10 He who loves his brother abides in the light, and there is no cause for stumbling in him.

> 1 John 4:21: And this commandment we have from Him: that he who loves God must love his brother also.

As you compare the epistles of 2 John and 1 John, the similarities are numerous and striking. Yet there seems to be little to no debate about 2 John being written only to believers. So why would one conclude that 1 John is written to a mixed crowd of believers and unbelievers when John uses virtually identical language for both? In addition, 3 John begins by using language and descriptions similar to his other two epistles.

> 3 John 1:1: The elder, to the beloved Gaius, whom I love in truth: 2 Beloved, I pray that you may prosper in all things and be in health, just as your soul prospers. 3 For I rejoiced greatly when brethren came and

> testified of the truth that is in you, just as you walk in the truth. 4 I have no greater joy than to hear that my children walk in truth.

No one seems to raise doubts that Gaius is an unbeliever who does not know or embrace the truth of the Gospel of Jesus Christ. So why should we raise doubts about the original recipients of 1 John in questioning the genuineness of their faith in Jesus Christ for salvation?

John's epistles clearly show that the readers of 1 John were believers, based on:

- John's identification with his Christian readers in his use of plural pronouns,
- his designations and descriptions of them, such as "little children,"
- his clear distinction of his readers from the unsaved Gnostic false teachers,
- the similar language used to describe the recipients of 2 John and 3 John who were unquestionably believers in Christ.

We can conclude with absolute certainty that John writes his first epistle with pastoral concern to those he considers to be true believers in Jesus Christ. John's original audience was not a mixture of believers and self-deceived hypocrites, who profess, but do not possess, eternal life. The identification of John's readers as believers is a critical piece of the exegetical puzzle for interpreting 1 John.

2. WHAT IS THE MAIN SUBJECT AND PRIMARY PURPOSE OF THIS EPISTLE?

Once again there are two conflicting perspectives regarding this pertinent question.

a. First John contains a series of tests to determine whether you truly possess eternal life or not.

An example of this viewpoint can be found in John MacArthur's book, *Saved Without A Doubt*, in which he claims that 1 John was written to provide a series of tests to determine whether professing believers are truly regenerate or self-deceived based on how they live.[1] The book contains a list of 11 "tests" to examine if a person is truly born again, which he claims are all found in 1 John. These 11 "tests of life" or marks of a true believer are expressed in the following questions:

1) Have you enjoyed fellowship with Christ and the Father?
2) Are you sensitive to sin?
3) Do you obey God's Word?
4) Do you reject this evil world?
5) Do you eagerly await Christ's return?
6) Do you see a decreasing pattern of sin in your life?
7) Do you love other Christians?
8) Do you experience answered prayer?

---

1. John MacArthur, Jr., *Saved Without a Doubt: How to Be Sure of Your Salvation* (Wheaton, IL: Victor, 1992), 67-91.

9) Do you experience the ministry of the Holy Spirit?
10) Can you discern between spiritual truth and error?
11) Have you suffered rejection because of your faith?

MacArthur and others partly draw this conclusion about the subject and purpose of 1 John based on a faulty interpretation of 1 John 5:13, which states:

> These things I have written to you who believe in the name of the Son of God, that you may know that you have eternal life, and that you may continue to believe in the name of the Son of God.

This is a wonderful verse on the assurance of salvation for believers. However, the tests-of-eternal-life view misuses it to teach that all of 1 John was written to provide the believer with assurance of eternal life. However, the problems with this faulty conclusion are many—both exegetically and doctrinally. Read on!

Exegetical and Doctrinal Observations on the Evidences of Regeneration View

This faulty conclusion is immediately seen to be problematic in light of the exegetical answer and conclusion from the first question about 1 John being written to believers, not unbelievers. In this epistle, the apostle John does not doubt the reality of his readers' salvation, nor does he put them to the "test" of true salvation, but instead he repeatedly reaffirms their salvation by calling them "my little children," "brethren," "beloved," and so forth. In addition, he explicitly states that they have eternal life, that they are of God, and that their sins are forgiven. It could not be any clearer that John is writing to believers in Christ who have already entered the family of God. He does not call into question their eternal salvation. He does not call them "my little children" or "brethren" and then ask them to prove it, just in case they are not really saved after all. He never expresses doubt about the reality or object of their faith being in Christ alone. Otherwise, John would be guilty of double-talk to the highest degree.

Second, this wrong conclusion for the primary subject and purpose of 1 John is further refuted exegetically by analyzing John's usage of the phrase, "These things I have written." This phrase is found four times in 1 John and each time it refers to the *immediately* preceding material.

> 1 John 1:4: And these things [1:1-3] we write to you that your joy may be full.

> 1 John 2:1: My little children, these things [1:5-10] I write to you, so that you may not sin. And if anyone sins, we have an Advocate with the Father, Jesus Christ the righteous.

> 1 John 2:26: These things [2:18-25] I have written to you concerning those who try to deceive you.

> 1 John 5:13: These things [5:9-12] I have written to you who believe in the name of the Son of God, that you may know that you have eternal life, and that you may continue to believe in the name of the Son of God.

Thus, it is without exegetical warrant to conclude that 1 John 5:13 is the summary statement for the entire epistle. I will discuss this further a little later.

Third, this wrong conclusion regarding the main subject and purpose of 1 John is also very problematic from a doctrinal standpoint. If what MacArthur and others are teaching were true, a believer in Christ could not know at the moment of faith in Christ that he or she was truly saved and possessed eternal life. Yet the Scriptures are very clear that no time delay is needed to check on one's "fruit," for God's promises can be trusted and the assurance of salvation can be enjoyed by every new-born child of God. Consider the following promises:

> John 3:16: For God so loved the world that He gave His only begotten Son, that whoever believes in Him should not perish but have everlasting life.

> John 5:24: Most assuredly, I say to you, he who hears My word and believes in Him who sent Me has everlasting life, and shall not come into judgment, but has passed from death into life.

These promises make it clear that the moment you place your faith in Jesus Christ you "ha[ve] everlasting life." Otherwise, you would have to wait to evaluate your life over time in order to see whether the various "tests of salvation" were true of you. But how much time is needed? One month? One year? Three years? Five years? The rest of your life? Regardless of the time element involved, your assurance of salvation would still be based upon your own biased self-perception of your daily walk, which may or may not be consistent with reality or God's evaluation of you.

Furthermore, since those who teach Lordship Salvation teach that assurance comes from looking at your life and works, they are really saying in essence, "If you want to know whether you are saved, get your eyes off Jesus Christ and His finished work alone, and instead look at your changing, daily condition and walk." Of course, they never say it so bluntly, for then it would be too obvious that they are teaching a works salvation. But in essence, they shift your focus from Christ's satisfactory work *for* you (which was "finished" on the cross) to Christ's sanctifying work *in* you (which is far from finished). This results in a shift from the truth of justification before God, which happens by one act of faith in Christ alone (Rom. 3:21-28; 4:1-5; 5:1), to a focus upon the truths of practical sanctification in time, which involve an ongoing walk of faith in Christ. According to this teaching, if you can walk sanctified enough, consistently enough, and fruitfully enough, then supposedly you can find the absolute assurance of your salvation. But Paul addresses such disastrous legalism in the book of Galatians, saying,

> 1 O foolish Galatians! Who has bewitched you that you should not obey the truth, before whose eyes Jesus Christ was clearly portrayed among you as crucified? 2 This only I want to learn from you: Did you receive the Spirit by the works of the law, or by the hearing of faith? 3 Are you so foolish? Having begun in the Spirit, are you now being made perfect by the flesh? 4 Have you suffered so many things in vain—if indeed it was in vain? 5 Therefore He who supplies the Spirit to you and works miracles among you, does He do it by the works of the law, or by the hearing of faith? (Gal. 3:1-5)

Following the logic of the Lordship Salvation teacher, you need to repeatedly self-evaluate your walk in light of the 11 tests of salvation or life supposedly found in 1 John. This is why many of those who hold this view are not absolutely sure of their own salvation until the day they die. And why would they have assurance of salvation, living under such performance-based, subjective criteria? They have taken their "eyes" off Jesus Christ and His finished work and put them on themselves and their walk. What a tragedy!

Let me repeat these 11 tests, but this time ask yourself the following questions to "test" yourself to see if you are truly saved.

- *Have you enjoyed fellowship with Christ and the Father?*

Questions: Can you honestly say you always enjoy fellowship with Christ and the Father? How often must you enjoy fellowship with Christ and the Father till you know that you *really* have eternal life? Every hour? Every day? Every week? Did you fail the test? How do you even really know? This approach to assurance leads to being tossed to and fro on a sea of personal subjectivity.

- *Are you sensitive to sin?*

Questions: Can you honestly say you are always sensitive to sin? How many sins? How often must you confess your sins to qualify? What about sins of ignorance? To what degree must you be sensitive till you know you are *really* saved? What about when you do not confess your sins, or do not realize that you have sinned? Can a Christian ever harden his heart and become insensitive to sin? If so, does that mean he was never saved? What about the Corinthian Christians whom God took home to Heaven because of their ongoing carnality? (1 Cor. 11:30-32) Were they never saved or were they saved but carnal (1 Cor. 3:1-4)? Did they fail the test of possessing true salvation? How carnal can you be, and for how long, before it is evident that you were never truly saved? One day? One week? One month? One year? How long? And did not some of the great believers recorded in Scripture fail to obey God's Word and became insensitive to sin? Did not King David commit adultery with Bathsheba, then scheme to have Uriah murdered and fail to confess his sins for many months? Was this proof that David was never saved? Or was this proof that David broke fellowship with God and lost the joy of his salvation for months, even though he was a genuine believer (Ps. 51:12)?

- *Do you obey God's Word?*

Questions: Can you honestly say you always obey God's Word? What Christian does? How often? In what areas? What about when you do not? How disobedient can a believer become before it is proof that he never *really* was saved? What about a believer who commits suicide? Or wrongfully divorces his or her spouse? Or what about the "sin unto death"? Or what about the lack of obedience in your life? Is this proof that you were never born again? All this self-analysis unfortunately focuses the believers on themselves and their daily walk and perceived spiritual batting average to know they are saved, instead of focusing on Christ's finished work with His promises that guarantee that "whoever believes in Him should not perish, but have everlasting life" (John 3:16).

- *Do you reject this evil world?*

Questions: Can you honestly say you always reject this evil world? How often do you really fail this test by your worldliness? To what degree must you reject the world? If you are a worldly believer, does this mean you were never *really* a believer at all? Aren't believers warned not to be contaminated by the world (James 1:27)? How often do you succumb to "the lusts of the flesh, the lust of the eyes, and the pride of life"? What about the sin of pride that dominates so many believers and churches? Does this mean they are not really children of God? Do they fail the test?

- *Do you eagerly await Christ's return?*

Questions: Can you honestly say you always eagerly await Christ's return? What about as a new believer, when perhaps you did not even know that He was going to return? Does this mean that you were never *really* redeemed? What if you hold to full preterism as your eschatology, believing that all prophecy was fulfilled by A.D. 70, and thus you do not wait for Christ to return? Does this mean you prove you are not saved? What if you go an hour without eagerly awaiting for it? How about a day? Or a week? Or a month? Did you fail this test of eternal life? Where on the sliding scale of subjectivity must you land to be fully assured of your own salvation?

- *Do you see a decreasing pattern of sin in your life?*

Questions: Can you honestly say you always see a decreasing pattern of sin in your life? Does the trend ever reverse? In what areas must this be true? How often? If this were true, then all genuine believers would be progressing in their Christian lives, never retrogressing. Has this always been true of you? What about when through the Word of God you become even more acutely aware of patterns of sin in your life? Does this mean that you were never *really* saved? If so, was Paul not saved in Romans 7 when he said that he was failing and frustrated in seeking to do God's will? How could this be true of a genuine believer, if one of the marks of true salvation is a decreasing pattern of sin in one's life? What if you started the Christian life well but ended poorly? Did you fail the test of true salvation?

- *Do you love other Christians?*

Questions: Can you honestly say you always love other Christians? If not, how often must you love them before you know you are *really* elect? All of the time? Some of the time? A little? A lot? Have you ever harbored bitterness and unforgiveness toward another Christian—perhaps for a period of time? How about in your marriage? How about toward your former spouse? Are you really saved if you only harbored bitterness for a day? What about two days? What about a week? What about a month? What about longer? How can you subjectively evaluate your salvation based on this introspective criterion? Is it not true that all believers have failed too many times to love others as Christ has loved them? Does this mean *they were never* truly saved by the grace of God?

- *Do you experience answered prayer?*

Questions: Can you honestly say you always experience answers to prayer? How often must you receive answers to prayer to know with certainty that you belong to the Lord? Daily? Weekly? Monthly? What about when prayer goes unanswered—perhaps for a long time? What about the many times were you failed to pray, let alone failed to experience answers to prayers? Did you fail the test of eternal life? Are you not *really* saved?

- *Do you experience the ministry of the Holy Spirit?*

Questions: Can you honestly say you always experience the ministry of the Holy Spirit? What exactly does that mean? Which ministry of the Holy Spirit must you experience before you are assured that you possess eternal life? While all believers today possess the Holy Spirit (Rom. 8:9), what about when you grieve the Spirit (Eph. 4:30)? What about when you quench the Spirit (1Thess. 5:19) instead of walking in the Spirit (Gal. 5:16)? Does this mean you were never saved? What if you are misled into some charismatic experience which you assume is wrought of the Holy Spirit, and thereby conclude that you must be saved because of this, only later to realize that your so-called "Holy Spirit" experience was not even in the Bible?

- *Can you discern between spiritual truth and error?*

Questions: Can you honestly say you are always discerning between spiritual truth and error? What about when you are not? Is it true that a genuine believer can never be misled doctrinally? If so, why do some believers not know the difference between grass and AstroTurf? What about new believers who are easily tossed to and fro by every wind of doctrine? And why then do some differ or change doctrinally? Is this proof they were never saved? In what areas of doctrine can a believer be undiscerning and still give proof that he is saved? All areas? Some areas? Major areas? How do you determine which are major versus minor areas of doctrine? Are we to conclude that children raised in Christian homes, who trusted in Christ at a young age, but later doubted God's Word, were never saved? Can Christians doubt a little but not a lot? Can Christians drift a little doctrinally but not a lot? Where is the line of "allowable doubt or drift" for the Christian before he concludes he was never truly saved? How often must you be discerning before you have proof in hand that you passed the test of life?

- *Have you suffered rejection because of your faith?*

Questions: Can you honestly say you always have been willing to suffer rejection because of your faith? Have you ever shrunk from giving your testimony to others? Have you ever loved the praise of men more than the praise of God? Have you ever passed on a witnessing opportunity because of the fear of man? Does this mean that you were never really born again? How often must you suffer rejection to be assured of eternal life? Once? Twice? Thrice? Are we to conclude that a person who is unwilling to suffer rejection by others under a certain circumstance, such as the real threat of family rejection or even martyrdom, was never really saved? Where do you draw the line?

Dear reader, by the time you are done evaluating yourself by these 11 "tests of life," you will have erased any absolute assurance of your salvation if you are honest with yourself. This is unless you are self-righteous enough to think that you might be saved because you measure up and make the grade.

Therefore, I would suggest that a better title for MacArthur's book would be: *Saved? With Many Doubts!* Perhaps this is why many who once knew they were saved through faith alone in Christ alone have lost the scriptural assurance that they have been saved by the grace of God. With stark honesty and self-evaluation in light of these 11 tests, who wouldn't?

Perhaps it is time to ask the Lordship Salvation teachers if they have 100-percent certainty that they are elect and have been saved by the grace of God? Can they truly say, "Yes, I have been saved without a doubt because I have passed all 11 tests of 1 John." Perhaps this is also why, when publicly asked about this, some of these very teachers have been honest enough to admit that they lack 100-percent assurance that they have eternal life. How does this square with 1 John 5:13, the very verse they claim teaches the purpose for the whole epistle of 1 John?

> 1 John 5:13: These things I have written to you who believe in the name of the Son of God, that you may know that you have eternal life, and that you may continue to believe in the name of the Son of God.

Ironically, the "test of salvation or eternal life" that is missing in MacArthur's book and the teaching of many is the only scriptural test that God actually requires. What exactly is it?

- ***Do you believe that Jesus Christ (God who became a man—the Son of God) died for your sins and rose again in order to give you eternal life?***

Is this not what it means to believe the Gospel of Christ?

> Romans 1:16: For I am not ashamed of the gospel of Christ, for it is the power of God to salvation for everyone who believes, for the Jew first and also for the Greek. 17 For in it the righteousness of God is revealed from faith to faith; as it is written, "The just shall live by faith."

And what exactly is the Gospel? It is contained in 1 Corinthians 15:1-4, which states:

> Moreover, brethren, I declare to you the gospel which I preached to you, which also you received and in which you stand . . . For I delivered to you first of all that which I also received: that Christ died for our sins according to the Scriptures, 4 and that He was buried, and that He rose again the third day according to the Scriptures.

And what is the one right response to the Gospel?

> 1 Corinthians 15:11: Therefore, whether it was I or they, so we preach and so *you believed*.

In addition, does not 1 John 5:9-13 actually make faith alone in Christ alone the real and only issue or condition in knowing that you have eternal life?

> 1 John 5:9-13 If we receive the witness of men, the witness of God is greater; for this is the witness of God which He has testified of His Son. 10 *He who believes in the Son of God* has the witness in himself; *he who does not believe God* has made Him a liar, because *he has not believed the testimony that God has given of His Son*. 11 And this is the testimony: that God has given us eternal life, and this life is in His Son. 12 He who has the Son has life; he who does not have

> the Son of God does not have life. 13 These things I have written to you *who believe in the name of the Son of God*, that *you may know that you have eternal life*.

Faith alone in Christ alone is the one and only condition to pass the "test of eternal life." Any teaching or theology that does not lead a believer to know with 100-percent certainty that they have eternal life cannot be from God and is not consistent with the true Gospel of salvation. Yet listen to the following story from one of the members of the local church where MacArthur pastors, and observe the confusion and destruction of personal assurance that the teaching of Lordship Salvation produces in a person's life. Keep in mind that MacArthur uses this as an illustration of the effects of his "strong preaching," saying "those who preach as they should will find some in their congregation plagued with doubt."[2]

> Dear John: I have been attending Grace church for several years, and as a result of a growing conviction in my heart, a result of your diligent preaching and seeming to be powerless against the temptations which arise in my heart and constantly succumbing to them, and talks with pastors and godly men about my growing doubts, has led me to believe I am not saved. How sad

---

2. John MacArthur, Jr., A Believer's Assurance: A Practical Guide to Victory over Doubt, Selected Scriptures, P17. See www.gty.org/resources/positions/P17/a-believers-assurance-a-practical-guide-to-victory-over-doubt

it is, John, for me to not be able to enter in because of the sin which clings to me and from which I long to be free. How bizarre for one who teaches in the Sunday School with heartfelt conviction, a trainer in Discipleship Evangelism, a seminarian at Talbot, a disciple. So many times I have determined in my heart to repent, to shake loose my want to sin, to forsake all for Jesus, only to find myself doing the sin I don't want to do and not doing the good I want to do. After my fiancée and I broke up, I memorized Ephesians as part of an all-out effort against sin, only to find myself weaker and more painfully aware of my sinfulness, more prone to sin than ever before, grabbing cheap thrills to push back the pain of lost love. Mostly in the heart, John, but that is where it counts and that's where you live. I sin because I'm a sinner.

I'm like a soldier without my armor and running across the battlefield getting shot up by the fiery darts of the enemy. I couldn't leave the church if I wanted to, I love the people, I'm enthralled by the gospel of the beautiful Messiah, I'm a pile of manure on the white marble floor of Christ, a mongrel dog that snuck in the back door of the King's banquet to lick the crumbs off the floor and by being close to Christians who are rich in the blessings of Christ, I get some of the overflow and I ask you to pray for me as you think best."

And he signed his name and then wrote a poem.

> I have no wings to Godward fly,
> but I slither quiet in slime.
> I have many tears to cry,
> but no repenting heart.
>
> There's no end to my sin,
> I have no hope to enter in,
> except by the blood of Jesus,
> only His precious blood pleases.
>
> O, God, a wretched man am I,
> lacking faith and trusting.
> Dearest Lord, hear my cry
> and give the Spirit renewing.
>
> If I could repent, I surely would
> and be Christ-like as I should,
> but no faith is in my breast
> and no assurance of eternal rest.
>
> My God, my God, forsake me not,
> but come to me and save me,
> take away my sinful rot
> and abide in me eternally.
>
> In You only is there hope,
> only You have power to cope.
> Quicken me and restore anew,
> I can't be a son without You.
>
> My God, my God, forsake me not,
> but come to me and save me."

Fresh Insights & Observations to Consider

Why does this man lack the assurance of eternal salvation? It is not because he does not know that, "I have no hope to enter in, except by the blood of Jesus, only His precious blood pleases." It is because while he knows of Christ's finished work on the cross, he looks for his assurance of Heaven in his imperfect walk and victory over sin (or lack thereof).

> Galatians 3:1: O foolish Galatians! Who has bewitched you that you should not obey the truth, before whose eyes Jesus Christ was clearly portrayed among you as crucified?

Dear reader, the issue in knowing that you have eternal life is simply this: Do you believe that Jesus Christ died for all your sins and rose again to give you eternal life and salvation as a gift solely of His grace through faith in Him? Tragically, this is the very issue about which people are *not* asked in MacArthur's book, *Saved Without A Doubt*. This is not one of the 11 "tests." Instead, people stumble at the simplicity of salvation by grace alone through faith alone in Christ alone. Instead their focus is unfortunately shifted from Christ to self, from His perfect and finished work to one's own imperfect daily walk—where no real absolute assurance can ever be found. Unfortunately, some believers in Christ have lost the *assurance* of their salvation through this erroneous teaching (though salvation can never be lost because believers are eternally secure). Yet it is also true that many others are *self-deceived* about the reality of their own salvation. But why? It is not because they acknowledge that they fail the 11 "tests of life" supposedly from 1 John. So why is it?

Many people wrongly assume they are born again because they have been baptized, or attend a church, or give money, or prayed a prayer, or walked an aisle, or asked Jesus into their heart, or made a commitment to Christ, or have sought to repent of their sins and surrender to the Lordship of Christ, and so on. But none of this is what the Bible requires to have eternal life. Consider the following verses written by the same author, the apostle John, regarding this very issue:

> John 1:12: But as many as received Him, to them He gave the right to become children of God, *to those who believe in His name*.

> John 3:14-18: And as Moses lifted up the serpent in the wilderness, even so must the Son of Man be lifted up, 15 that *whoever believes in Him* should not perish but have eternal life. 16 For God so loved the world that He gave His only begotten Son, that *whoever believes in Him* should not perish but have everlasting life. 17 For God did not send His Son into the world to condemn the world, but that the world through Him might be saved. 18 He *who believes in Him* is not condemned; but *he who does not believe* is condemned already, *because he has not believed in the name of the only begotten Son of God*.

Fresh Insights & Observations to Consider

John 3:36: He *who believes in the Son* has everlasting life; and *he who does not believe the Son* shall not see life, but the wrath of God abides on him.

John 4:42: Then they said to the woman, "Now *we believe*, not because of what you said, for we ourselves have heard Him and we know that this is indeed the Christ, the Savior of the world."

John 6:29: Jesus answered and said to them, "This is the work of God, that *you believe in Him whom He sent*."

John 8:24: "Therefore I said to you that you will die in your sins; for *if you do not believe that I am He*, you will die in your sins."

John 10:25-30: Jesus answered them, "I told you, and *you do not believe*. The works that I do in My Father's name, they bear witness of Me. 26 But *you do not believe*, because you are not of My sheep, as I said to you. 27 My sheep hear My voice, and I know them, and they follow Me. 28 And I give them eternal life, and they shall never perish; neither shall anyone snatch them out of My hand. 29 My Father, who has given them to Me, is greater than all; and no one is able to snatch them out of My Father's hand. 30 I and My Father are one."

> John 11:25: Jesus said to her, "I am the resurrection and the life. He *who believes in Me*, though he may die, he shall live. 26 And whoever lives and *believes in Me* shall never die. Do you *believe* this?"
>
> John 20:30-31: And truly Jesus did many other signs in the presence of His disciples, which are not written in this book; 31 but these are written that *you may believe* that Jesus is the Christ, the Son of God, and that *believing* you may have life in His name.

Observe how John in His Gospel gives no "tests of life" except whether one believes in Jesus Christ, the crucified and risen Son of God who came to give eternal life.

God has spoken and He has not stuttered that faith alone in Jesus Christ alone, as He is presented in the Gospel of grace, is the only condition to have eternal life and salvation. Yet so many today have a "hope-so" salvation that is based on faith in Christ PLUS their own human goodness or works, instead of a "know so" salvation guaranteed by the Scriptures that comes through faith in Christ PERIOD. So what does the Bible say about the condition for eternal salvation?

> Ephesians 2:8-9: For by grace you have been saved through faith, and that not of yourselves; it is the gift of God, 9 not of works, lest anyone should boast.

> Romans 3:28: Therefore we conclude that a man is justified by faith apart from the deeds of the law.

> Romans 4:5: But to him who does not work but believes on Him who justifies the ungodly, his faith is accounted for righteousness.

> Titus 3:5: not by works of righteousness which we have done, but according to His mercy He saved us.

Thus, many so-called "Christians" fail the real "test of eternal life," and they are not really saved because their faith is actually in their good works, making their salvation a reward for the righteous instead of God's gift to the guilty. This is why Jesus Christ said regarding the religious leaders of His day:

> Matthew 7:22-23: "Many will say to Me in that day, 'Lord, Lord, have we not prophesied in Your name, cast out demons in Your name, and done many wonders in Your name?" 23 "And then I will declare to them, 'I never knew you; depart from Me, you who practice lawlessness!'"

Observe carefully how these religious leaders were depending on Jesus Christ *plus* their religious works instead of on Christ alone to enter the kingdom of God. They were self-deceived and failed the only "test" of salvation. What a tragedy of monumental proportions! The apostle Paul explains this when he writes,

> Romans 9:30-33: What shall we say then? That Gentiles, who did not pursue righteousness, have attained to righteousness, even the righteousness of faith; 31 but Israel, pursuing the law of righteousness, has not attained to the law of righteousness. 32 Why? Because they did not seek it by faith, but as it were, by the works of the law. For they stumbled at that stumbling stone. 33 As it is written: "Behold, I lay in Zion a stumbling stone and rock of offense, And whoever believes on Him will not be put to shame."

Dear reader, is this true of you? Is your faith in Christ alone, or are you relying on your repentance from sins, your surrendering to Christ as Lord, your commitment to Christ, your perseverance and faithfulness in order to go to Heaven and eternal life? If your object of faith for eternal salvation is anything or anyone except Jesus Christ and His finished work alone, you will lack the absolute assurance of going to Heaven now or when you die, for you are interjecting yourself as part of the salvation equation (Christ's work + your work = salvation)—at least in your own thinking. Yet the Bible is clear when the Philippian jailer asked Paul and Silas the critical question, "What must I do to be saved?" They replied, "Believe on the Lord Jesus Christ and you will be saved" (Acts 16:30-31). Is that your answer to this important question? If you were to die and go to the gates of Heaven and Jesus Christ were to ask you why He should let you into His holy Heaven, how would you answer Him? Would you answer by referring to something that you have done for Christ, such as getting baptized, trying to love others, repenting of your sins, giving your life to Christ, asking God for forgiveness, surrendering to Christ's Lordship? Or would you reply by declaring the testimony of God and what Jesus Christ has done for you? Would you say something like:

> Lord, I am a hopeless, helpless, Hell-worthy sinner, who does not deserve to go into your holy Heaven. Nor do I believe that any of my good works can gain entrance there. But You, Lord Jesus, died for me and for all my sins, and You rose again to give me eternal life as a free gift of Your grace. And I have trusted in You alone to save me from the Hell I deserve to the Heaven I do not. In that moment when I transferred my faith from those things that cannot save me (my works, church sacraments, my commitment) and I trusted in You alone and what You did for me, you gave me the gift of eternal life and I have believed your promise. This is the only reason you should let me in, for it is solely by Your grace that I have been saved.

Do you see the critical difference between these conflicting and contrasting perspectives and approaches to salvation?

Now, regarding 1 John, do not misunderstand what the Bible states regarding the 11 godly traits. While believers *should* live lives that are characterized by godly, Christ-like characteristics, the Bible *does not guarantee* that all believers will live in this way. It is encouraged, but not guaranteed.

One sample should suffice to clarify this point. What about the lost soul who trusts in Christ as his Savior moments before he dies? This transpires because this person was willing to simply take God at His word by faith and believe the Gospel message. Is that person not truly saved, even though he lacked all 11 of these characteristics because he died moments later?

Furthermore, what about the carnal Corinthians, who were definitely members of the family of God and in Christ, yet were characterized by human wisdom and fleshly living, behaving like unbelievers?

> 1 Corinthians 3:1-4: And I, *brethren*, could not speak to you as to spiritual people but as to carnal, as to babes *in Christ*. 2 I fed you with milk and not with solid food; for until now you were not able to receive it, and even now you are still not able; 3 for you are still carnal. For where there are envy, strife, and divisions among you, are you not carnal and behaving like mere men? 4 For when one says, "I am of Paul," and another, "I am of Apollos," are you not carnal?

Paul states four times in four verses that these Corinthians were "carnal," yet he does not deny the reality of their salvation since he calls them "brethren" and "in Christ"—though they certainly were not living like it from day to day. According to the "tests of life" misinterpretation of 1 John, these carnal Corinthian Christians would have failed miserably the 11 supposed "tests of life" and would be viewed by many today as self-deceived unbelievers. Yet the Scriptures clearly reveal the reality of their position in Christ (1 Cor. 1:2; 12:13) and their being born-again (1 Cor. 4:15), justified members of the family of God (1 Cor. 6:11).

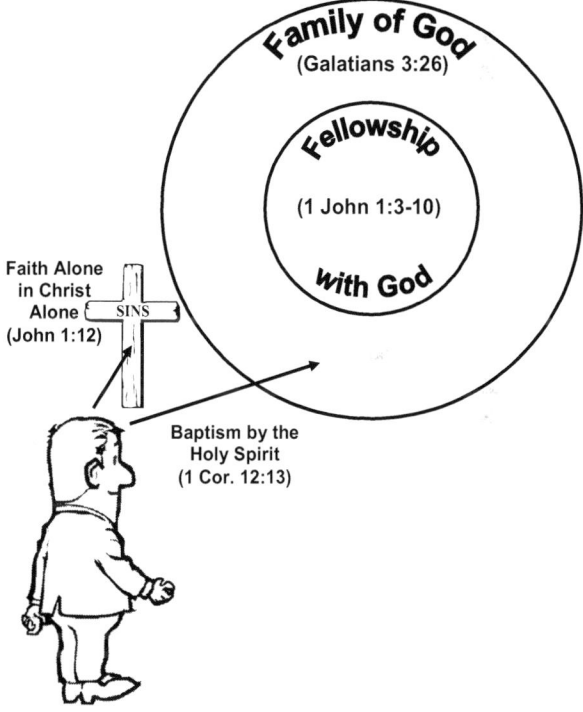

So is there another way to interpret 1 John besides the "tests of eternal life" view? Praise the Lord, there is! The second perspective regarding the primary subject and purpose of 1 John is:

b. First John gives the conditions and evidences of fellowship with God for the believer in Christ.

This is the perspective of the Scofield Study Bible, which states:

> THEME: First John is a family letter from the Father to His "little children" who are in the world. With the possible exception of the Song of Solomon, it is the most intimate of the inspired writings. The world is viewed as without. The sin of a believer is treated as a child's offence against his Father, and is dealt with as a family matter (1 John 1:9; 2:1). The moral government of the universe is not in question. The child's sin as an offence against the law had been met in the Cross, and "Jesus Christ the righteous" is now his "Advocate with the Father." John's Gospel leads across the threshold of the Father's house; his first Epistle makes us at home there.

In addition, the heading over 1 John 2:3 in the original Scofield Reference Bible reads, "The Tests of Fellowship: Obedience and Love." But what saith the Scriptures? Who is right?

Exegetical and Doctrinal Observations on the Evidences of Fellowship View

It is interesting to observe the contrast between the purpose statements for the Gospel of John versus the epistle of 1 John. John's approach in his Gospel narrative is to build a case for Jesus Christ's person and work throughout the book, and then hang the purpose statement on the back porch of the book, where he invites the reader to believe in Jesus Christ and receive eternal life:

> John 20:30-31: And truly Jesus did many other signs in the presence of His disciples, which are not written in this book; 31 but *these are written that you may believe that Jesus is the Christ, the Son of God, and that believing you may have life in His name.*

However, John's approach in 1 John, which was written to those who were already believers in Christ, puts the key to his primary subject and purpose on the front porch of the book. In his introduction John immediately states:

> 1 John 1:1-4: That which was from the beginning, which we have heard, which we have seen with our eyes, which we have looked upon, and our hands have handled, concerning the Word of life — 2 the life was manifested, and we have seen, and bear witness, and declare to you that eternal life which was with the Father and was manifested to us — 3 *that which we have seen and heard we declare to you, that you also may have fellowship with us; and truly our fellowship is with the Father and with His Son Jesus Christ. 4 And these things we write to you that your joy may be full.*

The apostle John makes it clear that he is declaring the truth about Jesus Christ so that believers may have "*fellowship* with us, and truly our *fellowship* is with the Father and with His Son, Jesus Christ." And why is he writing this epistle?

> 1 John 1:4: And these things we write to you that your joy may be full.

Could John be any clearer? Could he be any more upfront? He does not want his readers to miss his primary subject and purpose, yet so many still do! Do not stumble over the obvious. In contrast to the book of John which is primarily a large Gospel tract to unbelievers, 1 John declares the truth about Jesus Christ so that believers may have daily fellowship with God and Jesus Christ, with its evidences in their Christian lives (such as "full joy").

Second, this exegetical observation and conclusion for the primary purpose of 1 John being "fellowship" with God is further supported a few verses later when John writes:

> 1 John 1:6-7: If we say that we have *fellowship with Him*, and walk in darkness, we lie and do not practice the truth. 7 But if we walk in the light as He is in the light, *we have fellowship with one another*, and the blood of Jesus Christ His Son cleanses us from all sin.

This emphasis on fellowship with God is in keeping with the various descriptions given to believers as members of the family of God (the place of fellowship) as used by the apostle John. This includes such words as "born of God," "little children," and "brother."

First John is not about how to "enter" the family of God (like the Gospel of John – John 1:12-13; 3:1-21) but about how to enjoy "fellowship" with God and others as members of the family of God. Its purpose was not to be a personal litmus test about John's readers being believers or not since he was already convinced they were children of God. Instead, it is about whether these believers would walk in the light or in darkness, as evidenced by obedience and love.

Third, observe the contrast between Paul's use of "fellowship" and John's use. In 1 Corinthians, Paul speaks of believers in Christ being part of "the fellowship" *positionally* in Christ (1 Cor. 1:9), whereas 1 John talks about believers "having fellowship" *conditionally*. "The fellowship" (1 Cor. 1:9) is a noun phrase that refers to what all believers without exception are a part of because they are born again. However, to "have fellowship" is a verb phrase that has certain conditions attached to it—hence there are five conditional clauses in 1:5-10.

> 1 John 1:6: *If* we say that we have fellowship with Him, and walk in darkness, we lie and do not practice the truth.

> 1 John 1:7: But *if* we walk in the light as He is in the light, we have fellowship with one another, and the blood of Jesus Christ His Son cleanses us from all sin.

1 John 1:8: *If* we say that we have no sin, we deceive ourselves, and the truth is not in us.

1 John 1:9: *If* we confess our sins, He is faithful and just to forgive us our sins and to cleanse us from all unrighteousness.

1 John 1:10: *If* we say that we have not sinned, we make Him a liar, and His word is not in us.

The word "if" (*ean* + subjunctive) in each of its five occurrences in 1 John 1 introduces a third-class conditional clause, which means "if and you might or might not." This is clearly the "if" conditional clause of choice and volition with nothing assumed. Thus, a believer may either walk in darkness (1:6) or walk in the light (1:7). They may either confess their sins (1:9) or cover them (1:10). They have a choice to do either—moment by moment and day by day.

To "have fellowship" is a relational and conditional term, whether in reference to fellowship with God or with others. For though a couple may be married, this does not guarantee that they will always enjoy fellowship with one another. In fact, estrangement can occur in a marriage instead of fellowship. And when believers walk in the darkness of sin and falsehood instead of walking in the light of God's holiness and truth, they do not have fellowship with God (1:5-7). The same is true when they cover their sins instead of confessing them to God (1:9-10). Yet a willingness to walk by faith in the light of God's Word (v. 7a) combined with a willingness to confess one's sins to God when the Holy Spirit convicts (v. 9) produces fellowship with God and practical cleansing of sin, resulting in progressive sanctification in a believer's life (vv. 7b, 9b).

Fourth, from a doctrinal standpoint, would you even want to discuss with unbelievers how they can "have fellowship" with God when they are not even born again or part of the family of God? Unbelievers need to hear the Gospel first of all (1 Cor. 15:3-4). Then those who trust in Christ need to be instructed about how to "have fellowship" with God daily. Would you ever say to an unbeliever, "If we walk in the light" when they lack spiritual life and are unable to walk in the light? Would you ever require an unbeliever to "confess their sins" to be saved when the issue for eternal salvation is not a matter of confession of sins but of faith alone in Christ alone? This makes no biblical sense.

Fifth, it is important to note the heavy usage of the word "abide" in the book of 1 John. Remember that John was present with the Lord Jesus Christ when our Savior stated to His 11 believing disciples (Judas, the one unbelieving disciple had already departed – John 13:30):

> John 15:4-5: Abide in Me, and I in you. As the branch cannot bear fruit of itself, unless it abides in the vine, neither can you, unless you abide in Me. 5 I am the vine, you are the branches. He who abides in Me,

and I in him, bears much fruit; for without Me you can do nothing.

The apostle John never forgot those words, nor his daily need to "abide" in fellowship with Christ. It is the one requirement and only means to bear fruit for the Savior, including the fruit of the Spirit which is love. And John is passing on these instructions to these dear believers as well. Observe carefully in 1 John the following verses that clearly correspond to the Lord's teaching in John 15.

> 1 John 2:6: He who says he abides in Him ought himself also to walk just as He walked.

> 1 John 2:10: He who loves his brother abides in the light, and there is no cause for stumbling in him.

> 1 John 2:14: I have written to you, fathers, because you have known Him who is from the beginning. I have written to you, young men, because you are strong, and the word of God abides in you, [remember John 15:7] And you have overcome the wicked one.

> 1 John 2:24: Therefore let that abide in you which you heard from the beginning. If what you heard from the beginning abides in you, you also will abide in the Son and in the Father.

Fresh Insights & Observations to Consider

1 John 2:27: But the anointing which you have received from Him abides in you, and you do not need that anyone teach you; but as the same anointing teaches you concerning all things, and is true, and is not a lie, and just as it has taught you, you will abide in Him.

1 John 2:28: And now, little children, abide in Him, that when He appears, we may have confidence and not be ashamed before Him at His coming.

1 John 3:6: Whoever abides in Him does not sin. Whoever sins has neither seen Him nor known Him.

1 John 3:14: He who does not love his brother abides in death.

1 John 3:15: Whoever hates his brother is a murderer, and you know that no murderer has eternal life abiding in him.

1 John 3:17: But whoever has this world's goods, and sees his brother in need, and shuts up his heart from him, how does the love of God abide in him?

1 John 3:24: Now he who keeps His commandments abides in Him, and He in him. And by this we know that He abides in us, by the Spirit whom He has given us.

1 John 4:12: No one has seen God at any time. If we love one another, God abides in us, and His love has been perfected in us.

1 John 4:13: By this we know that we abide in Him, and He in us, because He has given us of His Spirit.

1 John 4:16: And we have known and believed the love that God has for us. God is love, and he who abides in love abides in God, and God in him.

The concepts of "abiding" and having "fellowship" go hand in hand in keeping with the main subject and purpose of 1 John.

It is also interesting to observe the following when comparing the Gospel of John and 1 John:

- The purpose statement of the Gospel of John: "that you might believe" (20:30-31)
- The purpose statement of 1 John: "that you also may have fellowship" (1:3-4)
- The usage of "believe" in the Gospel of John: 99 times
- The usage of "believe" in 1 John: 8 times
- The usage of the word *menō* ("abide") in John: 41 times in 21 chapters
- The usage of the word "abide" in 1 John: 24 times in 5 chapters

- The placement of the word "abide" in John which is predominately in John 15:1-10 which is spoken to believers only – 12 times

There is tremendous evidence to support that the apostle John relied heavily on the Lord's teaching in the Upper Room Discourse (John 13–17), and especially John 15, when writing 1 John. Again it is important to note that all the teaching portions of our Lord in the Upper Room occurred only when believers were present since "abiding" and "loving one another" are truths only for believers in Christ, not the unsaved.

Sixth, consistent with the believer's fellowship with God as the theme of 1 John, the use of the word "know" in certain contexts in 1 John refers to believers experientially knowing the Lord, not being born again. There are times when the word "know" in the Bible means more than the simple apprehension of knowledge, but to know intimately and personally, such as when "Adam knew his wife Eve and bore a son." It is one thing for the believer to know Jesus Christ as His Savior by faith alone, it is quite another to know Him intimately through daily fellowship with Him. Thus, we should not be surprised to read the following words in this epistle devoted to the subject of having fellowship with God the Father and Jesus Christ:

> 1 John 2:3: Now by this we know that we know Him, if we keep His commandments. 4 He who says, "I know Him," and does not keep His commandments, is a liar, and the truth is not in him.

Observe the similarity of these words to what John wrote in chapter 1 regarding fellowship with God.

> 1 John 1:6: If we say that we have fellowship with Him, and walk in darkness, we lie and do not practice the truth.

> 1 John 3:6: Whoever abides in Him does not sin. Whoever sins has neither seen Him nor known Him.

There are many exegetical and doctrinal reasons to conclude that 1 John was written to explain how believers, who are in the family of God, can enjoy daily fellowship with God and spiritual growth, with its godly evidences in their lives. These reasons are summarized as follows:

- the original recipients of 1 John were already believers in Christ
- the purpose of the book set forth in its introduction is fellowship with God (1:1-4)
- the usage of the word "fellowship" later in 1 John 1 that supports the stated purpose
- the five conditional clauses used in chapter 1 that relate only to a believer's walk
- the repeated usage of the word "abide" in 1 John in light of our Lord's teaching on fellowship with Him and fruitfulness as stated in John 15
- the usage of other "fellowship" terms in 1 John such as to "know" intimately

3. ARE THERE ANY EXEGETICAL INSIGHTS THAT CAN HELP YOU INTERPRET ACCURATELY 1 JOHN?

There are two exegetical insights that I would like to highlight that have helped me immensely in interpreting 1 John that I would ask you to examine and consider carefully.

The first exegetical insight relates to interpreting 1 John 1:5-10. After stating his purpose for writing this epistle to believers in Christ about having fellowship with God (1:1-4), the apostle John then begins to debunk three false claims about fellowship with God (1:6, 8, 10), as well as underscoring two required and related conditions to experience daily fellowship with God (1:7, 9).

What is noteworthy and vital to observe is the exegetical pattern John uses in this passage. In each clause, there is a distinct pattern of one condition or claim, followed by two consequences or results. Observe the following:

- Axiomatic truth: This is the message which we have heard from Him and declare to you, that God is light and in Him is no darkness at all. (1 John 1:5)

- False claim #1: If [third-class conditional clause] we say that we have fellowship with Him, and walk in darkness, [consequence #1] we lie, and [consequence #2] do not practice the truth. (1 John 1:6)

- Required condition #1: But [third-class conditional clause] if we walk in the light as He is in the light, [consequence #1] we have fellowship with one another, and [consequence #2] the blood of Jesus Christ His Son cleanses us from all sin. (1 John 1:7)

- False claim #2: If [third-class conditional clause] we say that we have no sin, [consequence #1] we deceive ourselves, and [consequence #2] the truth is not in us. (1 John 1:8)

- Required condition #2: If [third-class conditional clause] we confess our sins, [consequence #1] He is faithful and just to forgive us our sins and [consequence #2] to cleanse us from all unrighteousness. (1 John 1:9)

- False claim #3: If [third-class conditional clause] we say that we have not sinned, [consequence #1] we make Him a liar, and [consequence #2] His word is not in us. (1 John 1:10)

These exegetical observations have been helpful for me as I have read some very erroneous interpretations of this passage, especially 1 John 1:9.

A second exegetical insight that has helped me immensely to interpret 1 John with much more clarity and cohesiveness involves John's usage of anticipated assumption and insertion of previously stated truths in the epistle. Let me explain.

Many years ago it became plain to me that 1 John was written to believers in Christ about fellowship with God, not about tests of salvation. Yet I still struggled at trying to wrap my mind around some of the verses in 1 John. They seemed so difficult to interpret. They created doctrinal dissonance in my thinking in light of what I knew the Word of God taught in other passages. One example of this was 1 John 3:9.

> 1 John 3:9: Whoever has been born of God does not sin, for His seed remains in him; and he cannot sin, because he has been born of God.

What exactly was this verse stating? I knew that believers (whoever has been born of God) still sinned daily. Is that not why John wrote earlier, "If we confess our sins He is faithful and just to forgive us our sins and to cleanse us from all unrighteousness" (1 John 1:9)? Furthermore, what did 1 John 3:9 mean by "he cannot sin, because he has been born of God"? Believers cannot sin? Then why were the epistles written to believers if they "cannot sin"? And frankly, the explanation of many commentators that attempt to resolve this by claiming that a genuine believer does not have a *pattern of sin* did not sit well with me either. What about the carnal Corinthian Christians (1 Cor. 3:1-4)? What about the fact that God took some sinning Corinthian believers home to Heaven through divine discipline (1 Cor. 11:30-32)? What about believers I knew? How much sin does it take to constitute a *pattern of sin?* Three per day? Five? Ten? Twenty? All of this and more was problematic for me. (I will explain 1 John 3:9 later in this booklet).

When I was writing my first full-length book, *Shall Never Perish Forever*, I decided to tackle in the last third of the book approximately forty verses and passages that raise questions or act as proof texts for those who claim believers in Christ are not eternally secure. In addressing these verses, I needed to address 1 John 3:9, 15, and 5:16-17.

So I began to do my own exegetical study on these passages, recognizing context, examining content, and comparing Scripture with Scripture in order to ultimately arrive at a solid scriptural conclusion. Then I began perusing through many commentaries on this epistle, looking for any insights others have found that I needed to consider. It was during this process that I read a statement by Robert Yarborough that caught my attention and captured my interest. He wrote, "The latter theme, abiding, has come to be almost ubiquitous shorthand in 1 John. . . . John breaks no new ground; he just brings previously voiced convictions to bear."[3] Frankly, I was unsure what the word, "ubiquitous" even meant. So I looked it up in the dictionary which read, "existing or being everywhere, especially at the same time."[4] Merriam-Webster Dictionary defines ubiquitous as "seeming to be seen everywhere, often observed or encountered." Well, that was interesting, but was it true? Did the apostle John use "shorthand"

---

3. Robert W. Yarbrough, *1–3 John,* Baker Exegetical Commentary on the New Testament (Grand Rapids: Baker Academic, 2008), 202.

4. Dictionary.com.

seemingly everywhere throughout 1 John? I would soon find out.

In addition, I read in a commentary by D. Edmond Hiebert that gives one reason why John might use "shorthand" and make statements of this nature. Hiebert writes:

> While the Fourth Gospel is not without its difficulties of interpretation, it is well known that 1 John contains its due share of obscurities and ambiguities. . . . The fact that the epistle was addressed to readers familiar with the writer's teachings, as well as that the work was prompted by a sense of urgency in view of the crisis facing the readers, would help to account for these obscurities of expression.

By connecting these two observations, it made logical sense that if John knew his readers well, and if they were familiar with his teaching, then he could resort to "ubiquitous shorthand" and still be clearly understood.

Also, I was already aware how in everyday language we often employ an "ellipsis" in both verbal and written communication to indicate "an omission of a word or words that must be supplied to complete the sentence grammatically."[5] Let me illustrate. Suppose that you asked a friend, "Would you like to join us for supper Thursday night around 8 p.m. at Olive Garden restaurant? So can

---

5. Roy B. Zuck, *Basic Bible Interpretation* (Colorado Springs, CO: Cook, 1991), 152.

we plan on you?" Observe how much was omitted in the second sentence but still understood in light of the previous statement. You mentally inserted in the second sentence the following words, "So can we plan on you [for supper on Thursday night around 8 p.m. at Olive Garden restaurant]."

These omissions and needed insertions occur frequently in verbal and written communication. This can be seen in the following small sampling of scriptural examples.

> Psalm 8:3-5: When I consider Your heavens, [which are] the work of Your fingers, [when I consider] the moon and the stars, which You have ordained, what is man that You are mindful of him, And [what is] the son of man that You visit him? 5 For You have made him a little lower than the angels, And You have crowned him with glory and [You have crowned him with] honor.

> John 15:1-2: "I am the true vine, and My Father is the vinedresser. 2 "Every branch in Me that does not bear fruit He takes away; and every branch [in Me] that bears fruit He prunes [it], that it may bear more fruit.

> John 15:18: "If the world hates you, you know that it hated Me before [it hated] you.

> John 16:7-14: "Nevertheless I tell you the truth. It is to your advantage that I go

away; for if I do not go away, the Helper will not come to you; but if I depart, I will send Him to you. 8 "And when He has come, He will convict the world of sin, and of righteousness, and of judgment: 9 "[He will convict the world] of sin, because they do not believe in Me; 10 "[He will convict the world] of righteousness, because I go to My Father and you see Me no more; 11 "[He will convict the world] of judgment, because the ruler of this world is judged. 12 "I still have many things to say to you, but you cannot bear [them] now. 13 "However, when He, the Spirit of truth, has come, He will guide you into all truth; for He will not speak on His own [authority], but whatever He hears He will speak; and He will tell you things to come. 14 "He will glorify Me, for He will take of what is Mine and declare it to you.

Romans 6:11: Likewise you also, reckon yourselves to be dead indeed to sin, but [reckon yourself to be] alive to God in Christ Jesus our Lord.

Romans 8:3-7: For what the law could not do in that it was weak through the flesh, God [did] by sending His own Son in the likeness of sinful flesh, on account of sin: He condemned sin in the flesh, 4 that the righteous requirement of the law might be fulfilled in us who do not walk according to the flesh but [who walk] according to the Spirit. 5 For those who live according to the flesh set their minds on the things of the flesh, but those who live according to the Spirit, [set their minds on] the things of the Spirit. 6 For to be carnally minded is death, but to be spiritually minded is life and peace. 7 Because the carnal mind is enmity against God; for it is not subject to the law of God, nor indeed can [the carnal mind] be.

Galatians 5:16-17: I say then: Walk in the Spirit, and you shall not fulfill the lust of the flesh. 17 For the flesh lusts against the Spirit, and the Spirit [lusts] against the flesh; and these are contrary to one another, so that you do not do the things that you wish.

1 Corinthians 6:12-20: All things are lawful for me, but all things are not helpful [for me]. All things are lawful for me, but I will not be brought under the power of any. 13 Foods [are] for the stomach and the stomach [is] for foods, but God will destroy both it and them. Now the body is not for sexual immorality but [the body is] for the Lord, and the Lord [is] for the body. 14 And God both raised up the Lord and [the Lord] will also raise us up by His power. 15 Do you not know that your bodies are members of Christ? Shall I then take

the members of Christ and [shall I] make them members of a harlot? Certainly not! 16 Or do you not know that he who is joined to a harlot is one body [with her]? For "the two," He says, "shall become one flesh." 17 But he who is joined to the Lord is one spirit [with Him]. 18 Flee sexual immorality. Every sin that a man does is outside the body, but he who commits sexual immorality sins against his own body. 19 Or do you not know that your body is the temple of the Holy Spirit [who is] in you, whom you have from God, and [do you not know that] you are not your own? 20 For you were bought at a price; therefore glorify God in your body and [glorify God] in your spirit, which are God's.

2 Timothy 2:1-2: You therefore, my son, be strong in the grace that is in Christ Jesus. 2 And the things that you have heard from me among many witnesses, commit these [things] to faithful men who will be able to teach others also [these things].

2 Timothy 2:14-16: [You] Remind [them] of these things, charging [them] before the Lord not to strive about words to no profit, [but] to the ruin of the hearers. 15 [You] Be diligent to present yourself approved to God, [you be] a worker who does not need to be ashamed, [who is] rightly dividing the word of truth. 16 But [you] shun

profane and [you shun] idle babblings, for they will increase to more ungodliness.

These verses demonstrate that supplying a needed word or words to complete a thought or sentence is pervasive or "ubiquitous" not only in John's writing but throughout the Bible.

So with these observations and thoughts in mind, I read 1 John again, looking for his shorthand and insertions that would complete thoughts in light of previous statements he assumes that readers still remember. Here is an important section on 1 John 2:3-11 with John's omitted content restated in brackets:

> 3 Now by this we know that we know Him [intimately by fellowship with Him – 1:1–2:2], if we keep His commandments. [See 1:6-7]
> 4 He who says, "I know Him [intimately by fellowship with Him – 1:1–2:2] and [he] does not keep His commandments [1:6], [he] is a liar [1:6], and the truth is not in him. [1:10]
> 5 But whoever keeps His word [1:6], truly the love of God is perfected in him. By this we know that we are in [fellowship with – 1:3-7] Him.
> 6 He who says he abides in Him [John 15:1-7] [he] ought himself also to walk just as He walked.
> 7 Brethren, I write no new commandment to you, but [I write] an old commandment which you have had from the beginning.

> The old commandment is the word which you heard from the beginning.
> 8 Again, a new commandment I write to you, which thing is true in [fellowship with – 1:3, 7] Him and in [fellowship with – 1:3] you, because the darkness is passing away, and [because] the true light is already shining.
> 9 He who says he is [walking/abiding – 1:6-7] in the light [1:7], and [he] hates his brother, is [walking/abiding in – 1:6] in darkness [1:6] until now.
> 10 He who loves his brother [a fellow believer] abides in the light, and there is no cause for stumbling in him.
> 11 But he who hates his brother [a fellow believer] is [abiding – 2:10] in darkness and walks in darkness [1:6], and does not know where he is going, because the darkness has blinded his eyes.

This began to open up the epistle of 1 John for me and connect the dots exegetically as never before. It was a matter of paying attention to context, remembering previous statements that John made, and reinserting those statements based on context. Though I certainly did not want to be guilty of "adding" to the Word of God (Rev. 22:18), nor of "twisting" the Scriptures (2 Peter 3:16), I was convinced that there were good hermeneutical reasons for these growing interpretative conclusions. As I reflected on 1 John, its clear connection to the Upper Room Discourse (John 13–17), and especially the instruction to "abide in Christ" found in

John 15 and 1 John, another thought came to mind. Could it be that when John used the communicative method of "ubiquitous shorthand" he was simply following the Lord's example, the One who taught him the necessity of abiding? Notice how Christ uses "ubiquitous shorthand" in John 15:

> John 15:1-5: I am the true vine, and My Father is the vinedresser. 2 Every branch in Me that does not bear fruit He takes away; and every branch [in Me] that bears fruit He prunes, that it may bear more fruit. 3 "You are already clean because of the word which I have spoken to you. 3 Abide in Me, and I [will abide] in you. As the branch cannot bear fruit of itself, unless it abides in the vine, neither can you [bear fruit], unless you abide in Me. 5 I am the vine, you are the branches. He who abides in Me, and I in him, bears much fruit; for without Me you can do nothing [in terms of bearing fruit].

Yes, our Lord used "shorthand" and implied ellipsis when He spoke, and so does the apostle John. Notice the parallel with John 15 in the following verses:

> 1 John 3:24: Now he who keeps His commandments abides [John 15:4] in Him, and He [abides] in him [John 15:4]. And by this we know that He abides in us, by the Spirit whom He has given us.

> 1 John 4:13: By this we know that we abide in Him [John 15:4], and [that] He [abides] in us, because He has given us of His Spirit.

> 1 John 4:16: And we have known and believed the love that God has for us. God is love, and he who abides in love abides in God, and God [abides] in him.

These insights from Yarbrough and Hiebert, as well as examining 1 John in light of its "ubiquitous shorthand," threw the doors open for me to interpret more accurately 1 John as a whole, as well as some of the more difficult and perplexing verses that had bothered me over the years, such as 1 John 3:9, 15, and 5:16-18. Let's examine these next!

4. WHAT IS 1 JOHN 3:9 ACTUALLY SAYING?

> 1 John 3:9: Whoever has been born of God does not sin, for His seed remains in him; and he cannot sin, because he has been born of God.

Teachers offer various interpretations for many passages in the Bible with some interpretations being doctrinally correct and allowable but others doctrinally wrong and unacceptable. First John 3:9 is an example of a passage with widely varying views. Some interpreters see this passage as teaching that a person who sins at all is not born again. This "sinless perfection" view is extreme and held by only a few who are not honest with the text of 1 John, themselves, or the Lord, being self-deceived and failing to realize that we all still sin as believers in Christ. And they fail to read and grasp what John wrote two chapters earlier: "If we say that we have not sinned, we make Him a liar, and His word is not in us" (1:10).

Then there is the view held both by those who reject Lordship Salvation (yet seem to adopt some of its tenets) and those who embrace the false teaching of Lordship Salvation, who interpret this verse to mean that believers still sin but not as a pattern. If people continually sin as a pattern, then this supposedly means that they have never been born again. Those who hold this view appeal to the present tense of the phrases "does (*poieō*) sin" and "cannot sin (*hamartanein*)," claiming that these refer to habitually sinning or practicing sin. However, almost all major commentaries over the last fifty years on the Greek text of 1 John reject this interpretation that the born-again person does not habitually sin. This is because Greek grammarians recognize that the present tense verb can be used in a variety of ways and can refer to current action (a present or progressive present) and not necessarily to habitual, continual action (habitual present), depending on its context and the presence or absence of qualifying words.

Also, if people have been reading verse-by-verse through 1 John, they would have previously read in chapter 1 about the needed practice of confessing their sins in order to have fellowship with God (1:3-9). This is what verse 9 declares, "If we confess [present tense] our sins, He is faithful and just to forgive [present tense] us our sins and to cleanse us from all unrighteousness." In addition, if they keep reading on in 1 John, they will read in chapter 5: "If anyone sees his brother [a fellow believer] sinning [present tense] a sin which does not lead to death, he will ask, and He will give him life for those who commit sin not leading to death. There is sin leading to death. I do not say that he should pray about that." Thus, these two verses, 1:9 and 5:16, act as two bookends to clarify that those who are truly born again can commit (present tense) sin.

Also, from a practical standpoint, one commentator on the Greek text wisely remarks,

> A popular interpretation of these verses distinguishes between occasional sin (which every Christian commits) and a continuing lifestyle of sin, which a genuine Christian cannot pursue. Appeal is usually made to the present tense to support this view. The Greek present tense describes ongoing action (action in progress). The problem with this view is that the author of 1 John does not appear to distinguish anywhere else between a lifestyle of sin and occasional acts of sin. Also, to make such a significant interpretative point on the basis of the Greek tense alone is extremely subtle. One can only wonder whether John's readers would have gotten the point.[6]

---

6. W. Hall Harris, III, *1, 2, 3 John: Comfort and Counsel for a Church in Crisis* (n.p.: Biblical Studies Press, 2003), 143.

In addition, the view that claims "born again people don't habitually sin" simply doesn't hold water logically. From a practical standpoint, how many times must you sin a particular sin before it can be considered habitual or a pattern and then conclude that you are not born again? This view leaves one floating on a sea of subjectivity since it undermines the absolute assurance of one's salvation (which God offers all believers in His Word). Those who embrace this view subjectively evaluate how much sin they are committing or not committing to determine whether or not they are truly born again. What an endless spiritual squirrel cage of frustration! And if God can sovereignly prevent most sin in their lives (since they are elect) so that sin is not a "pattern," why doesn't God just prevent all sin in their lives? Obviously, there is a human element of choosing daily whether or not to appropriate God's grace resources in the process of sanctification, and such choices and patterns can fluctuate in one direction or the other.

Furthermore, what about godly believers in the Bible who sinned in flagrant disobedience against God, like David (adultery and murder), Abraham (lying), Peter (denying the Lord and hypocrisy with legalists), Moses (uncontrolled anger), and others? Were they not truly saved men? Again, how many sins constitute a pattern? How many times can you commit adultery before you are an adulterer? Or how many times can you murder before you are a murderer? Or steal before you are a thief?

Now, some will retort, "But they later repented of their sins." Yes, some did, thankfully, but not all did. For what proof exists that Solomon ever repented of his idolatry and worshipping of false deities? There is no record of any repentance in 1 Kings 11 which records his idolatry in later life, God's chastening rebuke, and his physical death. And what about the ongoing sins of the carnal Corinthian believers? The Scriptures clearly indicate that God disciplined "many" by physical death ("sleep") and took them home to Heaven because they were not repenting of their unfaithfulness and sins (11:30-32)? Others, like David, eventually repented of their sins to be restored to fellowship with God, but it took him many months. (Read 2 Samuel 11–12.)

Thus, we should reject the habitual-sin view based on Greek grammar, other verses in 1 John, numerous biblical examples, logical deduction, and its undermining of the scriptural doctrine of the absolute assurance of one's eternal salvation. So what is 1 John 3:9 actually teaching?

I appeal again to the context of the passage, the content of the verse, and to a comparison of Scripture with Scripture in order to arrive at the right biblical conclusion. The context of 1 John centers on the truths of fellowship with God (1:3-4), with the sanctification concept of "abiding" being prevalent in this epistle. Remember that the apostle John was present when Jesus Christ spoke these truths about the importance of "abiding" in John 15, and he never forgot them:

> John 15:4-5: Abide in Me, and I in you. As the branch cannot bear fruit of itself, unless it abides in the vine, neither can you, unless you abide in Me. I am the vine, you are the branches. He who abides in Me, and I in him, bears much fruit; for without Me you can do nothing.

With these verses in mind, it should not surprise us then to read 11 verses before 3:9 in 1 John 2:28:

> And now, little children, abide in Him, that when He appears, we may have confidence and not be ashamed before Him at His coming.

John addresses his readers as genuine believers in Christ ("little children") and commands them to "abide in Him." Why? Is it so they would not lose their salvation and arrive in Heaven? No! But so "that when He appears, we [the apostle John includes himself with these believers] may have confidence [having abided in Christ and been faithful and fruitful for Him] and not be ashamed [the opposite of confidence] before Him [at the Judgment Seat of Christ, cf. 1 Cor. 4:5; 2 Cor. 5:10] at His coming." When believers abide in Christ and bear fruit through the power of the Holy Spirit, others then will know that they are born of God because "everyone who practices righteousness is born of Him" (2:29).

First John 2:29 begins a section of Scripture that uses Jesus Christ as the Christian standard

Fresh Insights & Observations to Consider

and how believers reflect their abiding fellowship with Him by:

- manifesting practical righteousness to others since Jesus Christ is righteous (2:29)

- purifying themselves with the hope of His appearing and being like Christ since He is pure (3:2-3)

- living victoriously over sin by abiding in Christ since Christ came to take away our sins and in Him there is no sin (3:4-6)

So it should not shock us to read in 1 John 3:6 that "Whoever abides in Him does not sin. Whoever sins has neither seen Him nor known Him." In an epistle about the believer's fellowship with God and its practical outworking in obedience and love (2:3-11), we should not be surprised to read from an original apostle of our Lord about the importance of abiding in Christ. When believers are abiding in yielded dependence on the Vine, they are not at the same time guilty of sin (see also Galatians 5:16), though they still have much spiritual maturation to experience. Now, this present victory over sin is not because they have lost their sin nature through the new birth, for 1 John 1:8 declares, "If we say that we have no sin, we deceive ourselves, and the truth is not in us." Note that "sin" is both singular and a noun, in reference to the sin nature. Thus, to claim that we have no sin nature is to "deceive ourselves [not others like our spouse and kids], and the truth [regarding this issue] is not in us." One writer precisely observes,

> The habitual sin view is also ruled out by the context. In verse 5 John said that there is no sin in Christ. He clearly meant that there is absolutely no sin in Him. Then in the very next sentence he said that those who abide in Christ do not sin. He could hardly have meant that Christ sins not at all and those who abide in Him sin but not a lot. John's point is clearly that sin is never an expression of abiding in Christ. When we abide we do not sin at all.[7]

In contrast, 1 John 3:6 communicates that the believer who "sins has neither seen nor known Him." Both "seen" and "known" are in the perfect tense as state of being verbs that communicate intensity. This indicates intimately seeing and knowing a person. For example, the statement, "I'm seeing someone special," means more than visually observing someone with the naked eye. It speaks of a more intimate fellowship. The same is true of the biblical term "known" which can be used of possessing objective information (1 John 5:13) or of personal, intimate sexual or spiritual intercourse (Gen. 4:1; 1 John 4:8).

Next, the apostle John goes on to distinguish between the practical manifestations of righteousness to others by those believers who are abid-

---

[7]. Bob Wilkin, "Do Born Again People Sin?" *The Grace Evangelical Society News* (March 1990).

ing in Christ and those individuals who are not abiding. He writes, "Little children, let no one deceive you. He who practices righteousness is righteous, just as He is righteous" (3:7). This sounds very similar to 1 John 2:29 and how walking in the light and having fellowship with the Lord gives a practical manifestation to others of a believer practicing righteousness. Who, again, is the standard? Verse 7 reminds us "just as He is righteous." And who could potentially deceive the believers whom John addresses? The answer is false teachers who embraced an early form of Gnosticism from which they falsely concluded that physical matter was evil (1 John 1:1-3; 4:1-3) and that sin and God could somehow coexist in fellowship with one another (1:5). Therefore, the apostle John uses repeated absolute terminology throughout this epistle to expose this rank heresy so that believers would not be deceived.

In contrast to an abiding believer who practices righteousness, we then read, "He who sins is of the devil, for the devil has sinned from the beginning" (1 John 3:8). Obviously, the contrast between the manifestation to others of sin and righteousness in a person's life is striking.

Why does the believer who is abiding in Christ not sin at the same time that he is abiding? Why does the child of God who abides in Christ live in obedience to God's will (i.e. practice righteousness)? The answers are found in his spiritual birth and the new nature that he has received from God.

> 1 John 3:9: Whoever has been born of God does not sin, for His seed remains in him; and he cannot sin, because he has been born of God.

Through being born again ("Whoever has been born of God"), the believer does not sin (*when abiding in Christ* according to verse 6 in the immediate context), "for His seed [the new nature which comes from God through the new birth] remains in Him; and he [as a born again, new creation in Christ] cannot sin [as an expression of his new nature], because he is born of God." Some have interpreted "whoever has been born of God" to be the new nature which cannot sin. While this statement is true doctrinally, this verse does not say *"whatever* is born of God" but *"whoever* is born of God." It is referring to a person, not the nature in the person. It is referring to the one who has been born again. No believer ever commits sin as an expression of his new nature ("His seed"), yet the believer still sins when he yields to his sin nature, which still desires to reign as king in his life (Rom. 6:12). The sin nature reigns practically when believers fail to appropriate by faith (Rom. 6:11) Christ's victory over the sin nature at Calvary (Rom. 6:10), which they can claim because of their identification with Him in His death, burial, and resurrection (Rom. 6:1-6).

First John 3:9 obviously is a difficult passage regardless of what interpretation one embraces. It cannot contradict the multitude of clear passages in Scripture that teach the eternal security of the believer. But remember our previous observations about "ubiquitous shorthand"? Could this be the final solution to our exegetical problem? Could it be that John assumes that you will remember what he stated in verse 6 and insert this truth into verse 9? Consider the following when interpreting 1 John 3:6-9:

> Whoever abides in Him does not sin. Whoever sins has neither seen Him nor known Him. Little children, let no one deceive you. He who practices righteousness is righteous, just as He is righteous. He who sins is of the devil, for the devil has sinned from the beginning. For this purpose the Son of God was manifested, that He might destroy the works of the devil. Whoever has been born of God [and abides in Him, 3:6] does not sin, for His seed remains in him; and he cannot sin [when abiding in Christ, 3:6], because he has been born of God [with a new nature].

Thus, it is possible and even appropriate for us to understand John using the same stylistic shorthand and contextual assumptions to insert in 3:9 in light of his prior statement in 3:6. If this is true, the difficulty of 1 John 3:9 immediately clears up both exegetically and doctrinally. Consider these truths:

- When believers abide in Christ, will they have confidence before the Lord when He returns? YES!

- When believers fail to abide in Christ, will they be ashamed before Christ at His coming? YES!

- When believers walk by faith in fellowship with the Lord, do they practice righteousness toward others, reflecting Christ who is righteous? YES!

- When believers do not walk by faith in fellowship with the Lord, do they practice righteousness toward others and reflect Christ who is righteous? NO!

- When believers have the hope of Christ's appearing abiding in them, do they purify themselves as Christ is pure? YES!

- When believers do not have the hope of Christ's appearing abiding in them, do they purify themselves as Christ is pure? NO!

- When believers abide in yielded dependence upon the Lord as their Life, do they at the same time sin? NO! Why? Because Christ has come to take away sin and in Christ there is no sin.

- When believers fail to abide in Christ, do they fail to see and know Christ in intimate fellowship with Him? YES!

- When believers who are born again abide in Christ, do they sin? NO! Why? Because they have God's seed remaining in them (the new nature) via the new birth which is incapable of sin.

Fresh Insights & Observations to Consider

- Does 1 John 3:9 teach that a sinner who is born again is incapable of practicing sin? NO!

- Does 1 John 3:9 teach that if a so-called believer does practice sin that he was never truly born again? NO!

- Does 1 John 3:9 teach that believers can ever lose their eternal salvation? NO!

- Does 1 John 3:9 teach that all genuine born-again believers will persevere in faith and holiness all the days of their lives or else they were never truly born again? NO!

- Is 1 John 3:9 a difficult verse to interpret? YES!

- Is it possible that John used "shorthand" at times in this epistle and that he assumed his readers would understand verses in light of context, previous statements, and appropriate insertions? YES!

- Does the Bible correctly understood ever contradict itself? NO! Nor does it here! Praise the Lord!

5. WHAT IS 1 JOHN 3:15 TEACHING?

> 1 John 3:15: Whoever hates his brother is a murderer, and you know that no murderer has eternal life abiding in him.

At first glance this is a perplexing verse indeed that is subject to various interpretations. I would again ask that you be like the Bereans (Acts 17:10-11) and consider what I have written and search the Scriptures to make sure these things are so. This epistle addresses the believer's fellowship with God (1:3-4) and related truths, not the condition or tests of salvation. This is taught by John in light of the incipient Gnosticism infiltrating the early Church. As a result, John begins this epistle by describing the humanity of Jesus Christ in empirical terms, bookended by the reality that He is "from the beginning" (v. 1) and "eternal life" and was "with the Father" (v. 2), which both emphasize His deity.

> 1 John 1:1-2: That which was *from the beginning,* which we have *heard,* which we have *seen* with our eyes, which we have *looked upon*, and our *hands have handled*, concerning the Word of life — *the life was manifested*, and we have *seen*, and bear witness, and declare to you that *eternal life* which was *with the Father* and was manifested to us.

One of the key terms in 1 John is the concept of "abiding" in Christ taken from John 15 which describes a believer's fellowship and fruitfulness by and for Jesus Christ.

Fresh Insights & Observations to Consider

In contrast to loving a fellow believer, which is a reflection of abiding in Christ and a test of fellowship, we observe in 3:15 that "whoever hates his brother is a murderer." Notice that this person hates "his brother," which indicates he himself is a believer and is failing to love another believer. Therefore, he is not abiding in Christ while this is true. God likens this hating of one's brother to being a "murderer." Why? It is because God does not need to see the action of murder to discern the attitude of hatred that underlies the sinful action which is its consequence. This is similar to the statements of our Lord about the sinful attitudes of unrighteous anger and unrestrained lust that God considers "murder" and "adultery" (Matt. 5:22-28).

But this raises the question, what does it mean that "you know that no murderer has eternal life abiding in him"? Does it mean that if you murder, you cannot go to Heaven? No, for Saul (Paul) was the chief of sinners, yet He was given eternal life by God's grace and mercy when he trusted in the Savior (1 Tim. 1:15-16).

Does it mean that if you ever murder, it proves you were never saved? To arrive at this erroneous interpretation would cause you to conclude that both Moses and David were never saved since both were guilty of murder. And if that was the right conclusion, why would Peter exhort *believers* not to suffer as murderers (1 Peter 4:12-16)?

Does it mean that genuine believers never "practice" hatred though it can occur on occasions? This creates the problem of how many times you can sin before it is constituted a "practice," especially as it relates to "murder" in the context. And what about the sin of bitterness that oftentimes is a bed partner with hatred that believers are also certainly guilty of (Heb. 12:15)? Or does it mean that you could have been saved, but now you have forfeited it and lost your eternal salvation because you committed murder? If this was possible, how did this sin somehow fail to be paid in full by the blood of Christ? And how could this specific sin have escaped the forgiveness of all sins (past, present, and future) that a sinner receives when he comes to Christ by faith (Col. 2:13)?

The solution to interpreting this problem in 1 John 3:9 is wrapped up in the phrase "eternal life abiding in him." The phrase "eternal life" is a reference to Jesus Christ as introduced at the beginning of this epistle,

> 1 John 1:2: We . . . declare to you that eternal life which was with the Father and was manifested to us.

Jesus Christ is referred to again as "eternal life" at the end of John's letter.

> 1 John 5:20: And we know that the Son of God has come and has given us an understanding, that we may know Him who is true; and we are in Him who is true, in His Son Jesus Christ. This is the true God and eternal life.

The phrase "abiding in him" hearkens back to the words of our Lord in the Upper Room Discourse (John 13-17) that John repeatedly draws upon in this epistle. In the context of a mutual personal fellowship with Christ and vice-versa, Christ clearly stated, "Abide in Me and *I in you*" (John 15:4). Likewise, in 1 John 3:6, the aged apostle wrote, "Whoever *abides in Him* does not sin" at the same time because of the purpose of Christ's coming and His own sinlessness as a person (3:5). Thus, 1 John 3:15 is simply reiterating this same truth from the opposite angle that, "Whoever [a believer] hates [a failure to love] his brother [a fellow-believer] is a murderer [as God perceives the heart], and you know that no murderer [the believer who is hating his brother] has eternal life [Jesus Christ] *abiding in him* [by way of Christ's fellowship]." In other words, when a believer hates a fellow-believer, he is not at the same time abiding in Christ and having fellowship with Christ, nor is Christ abiding in him and having fellowship with him. The two are mutually exclusive. Once again John is destroying the incipient Gnostic's false teaching that light and darkness coexist with God (1:5), which would have a devastating effect upon these believers and would compromise their walk with a holy God (1:6-7).

Thus, light and insight is shed on 1 John 3:15 by examining again the general and specific *context* of 1 John 3, followed by observing the *content* of this verse as it relates to the key words "eternal life" (1:1-2) and "abiding in him," along with *comparing Scripture with Scripture* such as John 15, 1 John 3:6, and other passages that clearly indicate what this verse cannot be stating. First John 3:15 is consistent with the overall thrust of the epistle of 1 John which teaches that a believer who is walking in the light abides in Christ and has sweet fellowship with Him (who is love), resulting in love and not hatred for fellow believers. Conversely, when you know that a believer hates his brother, you know he is not abiding in Christ's fellowship, nor is Jesus Christ (eternal life) having fellowship with Him.

There is no loss of eternal salvation taught in this verse, but did you really expect to find that doctrine taught in this passage since the Bible correctly understood never contradicts itself? Perhaps not, but you may have wondered like I did for years, "What exactly is 1 John 3:15 teaching?" Hopefully now you know!

6. WHAT IS 1 JOHN 5:16-17 TEACHING?

> 1 John 5:16-17: If anyone sees his brother sinning a sin which does not lead to death, he will ask, and He will give him life for those who commit sin not leading to death. There is sin leading to death. I do not say that he should pray about that. 17 All unrighteousness is sin, and there is sin not leading to death.

Are these verses indicating that a believer can commit a sin that leads to spiritual or eternal death and therefore the loss of eternal salvation? The *general context* of 1 John deals with the reality that, though the believer in Christ can never lose eternal life, he must abide in fellowship with

Fresh Insights & Observations to Consider

Christ since this fellowship can be lost. The *immediate context* of 1 John 5:14-15 gives divine assurances to answered prayer when asked according to God's will. With these facts in mind, verses 16 and 17 now give a tangible illustration of this.

So let's begin to analyze this passage by observing the *content* of these verses which is fraught with exegetical difficulties and differences among Bible commentators because of John's loose Greek constructions, obscure meanings, and theological imports. Let me add my conclusions to the mix for your studied and prayerful consideration. The word "if" (*ean* + subjunctive = third-class condition) indicates that the following event is a possibility. The phrase, "if anyone sees his brother sinning a sin," reveals that the apostle John is talking about one believer ("if anyone" – intercessory prayer is available to all) observing ("seeing") another believer ("brother") "sinning" (present tense – present active participle of *hamartanō*, indicating that this sinning is deliberate and it appears externally as overt sin, not just a suspicion). When John refers to "a sin" that a believer observes another believer sinning, the nature or description of any particular sin is not given; nor is there the definite article before the word "sin." This indicates that John is not singling out a specific sin but probably the quality of a state of rebellion (see 1 John 3:4). The phrase, "a sin," clearly indicates that believers still sin, sometimes with no regard to whether they are seen or not by others (reflecting hard-hearted carnality) and that some of their sins are clearly observed by other believers (and it should probably be assumed by unbelievers as well). What are the results of this believer "sinning a sin"? Two possible consequences are stated. First, it could be that the sin "does not lead to death." This is best understood to be a reference to "physical" death? Why? It is because:

- there are several cases in Scripture where God disciplined His children via physical death, such as Ananias and Sapphira (Acts 5), many of the Corinthian Christians (1 Cor. 11:30), and others. Thus, physical death is a viable option for "death" in this verse.

- the sinner who believes the record of God concerning Jesus Christ has "passed from death into life" spiritually (John 5:24). Thus, "spiritual" death (Eph. 2:1) is eliminated as an option.

- the believer has "eternal life" and shall not come into condemnation later (John 5:24), so that he can "know" that he "has eternal life" (1 John 5:13). Thus, "eternal" death is removed as an option.

- while the believer can still experience "temporal" death as a loss of fellowship with God because of carnality (Rom. 8:6, 13; 1 Tim. 5:6; James 1:15), this verse says that this sin "does not lead to death." However, James 1:15 is clear that "when desire has conceived, it gives birth to sin; and sin, when it is full-grown, brings forth death." Sin always leads to a breakage of fellowship with the Father for the believer, but this sin in 1 John 5:16 "does not lead to death." Thus, physical death is the only good option exegetically and doctrinally.

The second possible consequence when a believer sins a sin is that it leads to physical death via divine chastening, as the passage says, "there is a sin resulting in death" (5:16b).

How should a believer respond when he sees a brother sinning a sin that does not lead to physical death and the apparent early home going of this rebellious child of God? He should specifically intercede for him in prayer (he should "ask"). What specifically should he ask for? He should ask for his spiritual restoration to fellowship with God. (This must mean "life" in contrast to temporal "death," for how can God answer his prayer and give the sinning believer "life" unless he is dead in some sense though not physically?) If the believer will pray for the sinning believer this way, the verse promises, "and He" (God) "will give him life" (an answer to his prayer for other believers) "for those who commit sin not leading to [physical] death." Earlier in this epistle 1 John 1:9 made it abundantly clear that when we as believers sin, we need to "confess our sins" and appropriate God's fellowship forgiveness. And 1 John 2:1-2 indicates that while God does not desire for His children to sin, they still do and Jesus Christ ever lives to make intercession for them as their righteous advocate when they sin.

First John 5:16 now highlights for us how we as believers are to respond when observing another believer sinning a sin that does not result in physical death. The answer is to engage in intercessory prayer for other believers who are sinning which would be consistent with praying according to God's will (vv. 14-15) and genuine love for the brethren (a key concept throughout 1 John as found in 3:11, 23; 4:7, 11-12). What, then, can we anticipate resulting from our intercession for the sinning believer? The answer at the end of verse 16 is "and He" (God) "will give him" (the sinning believer) "life" (restoration to fellowship from his temporal death and access to an abundant life; see Luke 15:24) "for those" (this anticipates other sinning believers are also in view and prayed for) "who commit sin not leading to [physical] death." Yes, there is tremendous value in praying out of love for fellow believers, even the sinning ones. This also means that you need to be humble enough to recognize that at times others should also pray for you!

Having explained the right loving response when observing a believer sinning a sin in rebellion towards God, John explains what the believer's response should *not* be toward his fellow believer. He states, "There is sin leading to [physical] death. I do not say that he should pray about that." The New American Standard Bible translates this sentence, "There is a sin leading to death; I do not say that he should make request for this." In other words, when we observe a fellow believer sinning a sin, do not pray that God would divinely discipline him with physical death (though we may be tempted to do so).

Like a good expositor and teacher, the apostle John next anticipates the reactions of his audience to his previous comments and seeks to clarify any misconceptions that could result. Next John anticipates that some people will make light of sin as inconsequential since it does not result in physical death. Thus, he adds, "all unrighteousness is sin" in God's eyes, which is probably another rap against the Gnostic's false teaching which downplayed the significance of sin in the believer's life. He then ends by underscoring that "there is a sin not leading to [physical] death," though it still results in a death-like existence of broken fellowship with God unless the believer confesses it as sin to God and his fellowship with God is restored (1 John 1:9). Hiebert accurately writes, "All sin is serious but not all is hopeless and beyond the reach of Christian intercession; this leaves a standing challenge to brotherly intercession."[8]

Whether one agrees with all my interpretative conclusions or not, one thing is strikingly clear. This passage does not indicate that a brother (believer) who sins a sin (whether leading to physical death or not) ceases to be a "brother" in the forever and forgiven family of God. His eternal salvation is never in jeopardy of loss or forfeiture. And what else would we expect from an epistle like 1 John that is devoted to explaining the truths of fellowship with God as a believer against the

---

8. D. Edmond Hiebert, *The Epistles of John* (Greenville, SC: Bob Jones University Press, 1991), 263.

backdrop of the false teaching of the Gnostics. Thus all believers, whether immature or mature, walking in the light or in darkness, are repeatedly addressed in 1 John by such terms as those who are "born" of God (2:29; 3:9 [twice]; 4:7; 5:1, 18 [twice]), or as "little children" (*teknia* – a term used of all believers in 2:1, 12, 28; 3:7, 18; 4:4; 5:21-22) or as "beloved" (*agapētoi* – a term used of all believers who are especially loved by God in 2:7; 3:2, 21; 4:1, 7, and 11).

John is not calling into question the standing of these believers before God as born-again children of God, but on the contrary he repeatedly affirms it. Yet John is challenging and instructing these believers in this epistle with the parent-child motif and its appropriate language about their daily fellowship with their heavenly Father and His Son, Jesus Christ, which results in obedience to God's will and love for fellow believers. Once you have been born into a family are you not the child of your parents forever whether you obey them or not? That parent-child relationship is settled forever and unchangeable. Yet it remains to be seen if you will walk in daily fellowship with your parents or not. A failure to do so never jeopardizes your once-and-for-all physical birth, but it does affect the quality and consistency of the fellowship you will enjoy with them, or the loving discipline they may need to exercise in your life. Did not the Holy Spirit so direct the writers of Scripture, and in particular the apostle John, to utilize the concepts of the never-to-be-repeated new birth that can never be lost or forfeited versus daily, repeated fellowship with God that can be lost or forfeited so as to keep clear these important scriptural truths? I believe the biblical evidence overwhelmingly supports this conclusion.

Dear readers, when you let the Scriptures speak for themselves, they harmonize wonderfully. You need not force or manipulate verses to reconcile them since there is no need to reconcile friends. And once again we observe the Word of God exalting the Son of God and the grace of God which is ever flowing to you and me!

7. WHAT HAVE WE LEARNED ABOUT INTERPRETING 1 JOHN AND WHAT DIFFERENCE DOES IT MAKE?

It has not been my intent in this booklet to give a commentary on every verse in the tremendous epistle of 1 John. But it has been my desire to make some critical observations that can shed light on the correct interpretation of this epistle as a whole, as well as individual difficult verses in particular. What have we observed?

- That the original readers of 1 John were believers in Christ, not the unsaved or a mixed group.

- That the primary purpose of 1 John is to instruct believers about having fellowship with God in their daily walk, not tests to determine if they truly possess eternal life.

- That the predominant evidences of a believer's fellowship with God are obedience to His will and a genuine love for other believers.

- That the backdrop to this epistle was the inroads of false teachers into the Church, who taught a form of dualistic Gnosticism that could adversely influence these believers in Christ to accept a mixture of sin and fellowship with God view.

- That the apostle John knew his readers well and vice-versa, allowing him to use "ubiquitous shorthand" in his writing and still be understood.

- That John expects these believers to remember what he taught them earlier in his epistle and mentally reinsert the necessary word or words to properly complete the thought or sentence.

- That 1 John 3:9, 15, and 5:16-18 all deal with the believer's abiding fellowship with Christ and vice-versa, and the impossibility of sinning at the same time.

So what difference does all of this make? The proper interpretation of 1 John:

- Distinguishes between entering the family of God and possessing eternal life by faith alone in Christ alone (Gospel of John) versus having fellowship with God and Jesus Christ after you have been born again into the family of God (1 John).

Fresh Insights & Observations to Consider

- Allows believers in Christ to possess or regain the absolute assurance of their eternal salvation at the moment of faith alone in Christ alone based upon the Word of God and the finished work of Christ at Calvary (5:9-13), instead of looking for that assurance based upon their subjective perception of their fluctuating walk with Christ which the "tests of life" view requires.

- Clarifies important truths about the believer's walk and fellowship with Christ as it relates to walking in the light (1:7) and the confession of sins (1:9).

- Debunks false claims regarding the believer's fellowship with God as it relates to sinning at the same time (1:7), not having a sin nature (1:8), or the covering of sin (1:10).

- Underscores that obedience and love in the believer's life will indicate whether he or she is abiding in Christ or not.

- Recognizes that whoever is born of God does not sin when abiding in Christ, nor is sin an expression of his new nature (1 John 3:9).

Frankly, I have never heard of so many believers in Christ as I have in the last few years that are struggling with the assurance of their salvation because of the wrong interpretation of 1 John and the "tests of life" self-analysis view. This erroneous interpretation of 1 John robs honest, self-evaluating people of the assurance of knowing they have eternal life as their focus shifts from Christ's finished work *for* them on the cross and resurrection to Christ's work *in* them which is far from perfect and can be resisted. And though I do not want to give a false assurance to one who has a faith in Christ PLUS view of salvation since the Bible teaches that salvation is all by grace apart from our works (Eph. 2:8-9), nor do I want believers in Christ alone as Savior to be tormented with a lack of absolute assurance when God wants them to have it, for 1 John 5:11-13 promises:

> 11 And this is the testimony: that God has given us eternal life, and this life is in His Son. 12 He who has the Son has life; he who does not have the Son of God does not have life. 13 These things I have written to you who believe in the name of the Son of God, that you may know that you have eternal life, and that you may continue to believe in the name of the Son of God.

Made in United States
Troutdale, OR
11/27/2024

25404237R00058